SAMARIA IN AHAB'S TIME

HARVARD EXCAVATIONS AND THEIR RESULTS

SAMARIA IN AHAB'S TIME

HARVARD EXCAVATIONS AND THEIR RESULTS

WITH CHAPTERS ON THE POLITICAL AND RELIGIOUS SITUATION

BY

J. W. JACK, M.A.

AUTHOR OF
'THE DATE OF THE EXODUS IN THE LIGHT OF EXTERNAL EVIDENCE'

Edinburgh: T. & T. CLARK, 38 George Street
1929

PRINTED IN GREAT BRITAIN BY
MORRISON AND GIBB LIMITED
FOR
T. & T. CLARK, EDINBURGH
LONDON: SIMPKIN, MARSHALL, HAMILTON, KENT AND CO. LIMITED
NEW YORK: CHARLES SCRIBNER'S SONS

PREFACE

The object of the writer in issuing this book is not so much to give a concise account of the Harvard excavations at Samaria, in so far as they throw light on the history of Israel, as to state certain significant conclusions which seem to be based upon them. So much has been written on the Old Testament that another book, however small, on the subject may seem superfluous, but the excavations disclose important new facts derived from the best of all historical sources, the pick and the spade. They give us fresh knowledge of Israel in Ahab's time, and much enlightenment on the northern Semitic alphabet and other matters. A new picture of Samaria, with its royal and civil administration, takes the place of the old long-familiar one, and supplements the scanty historical material in the Biblical record.

The researches of scholars in Old Testament literature and wider Semitics have afforded us more information in the last fifty years than were gained in all the preceding ages. Yet it is little compared with all that lies untouched. There are still huge gaps in the history of Israel, and on these and other very important matters we can only await the excavator's spade. Unfortunately, in spite of the valuable work of the Harvard archæologists, only a small part of the space within the walls of Samaria has been laid bare. Searchers might yet light on the royal tombs, in which so many Israelite kings rest, or on the site of the temple of Melḳart, the Tyrian Baal, or on the ruins of the temple of Astarte, which was still in existence when the town was destroyed. For the magnificent work already accomplished, however, the Harvard excavators have earned the gratitude of all Biblical scholars.

The writer desires to tender his thanks to Harvard University, and especially to Professor David G. Lyon, honorary curator of the Semitic Museum, for permission to use the excavators' reports, together with several of the plates and plans. It would be impossible for the writer to enumerate all the other works to which he has been indebted in forming his conclusions, but a few of those consulted have been mentioned in the footnotes. He feels specially indebted to Professor René Dussaud, Dr. W. F. Albright, and other Semitic authorities for helpful comments on the subject.

If these pages should awaken further interest in the important questions discussed, the writer will feel amply rewarded for his trouble.

J. W. J.

February 1929.

NOTE

In the transliteration of names, certain letters, often confused in English but distinct from each other in Semitic languages, are differentiated as follows:

h is used for the ordinary hard breathing, *ḥ* for the guttural one (Arabic ح, Hebrew ח), and *ḫ* for the harder guttural *kh* (except in a few names where the latter has become more usual).

ḳ is used for the emphatic *k* (Arabic ق, Hebrew ק), as distinct from the ordinary one (Arabic ك, Hebrew כ).

ṣ represents the hard Semitic sibilant (Arabic ص, Hebrew צ).

sh is generally used in Babylonian words instead of *ś*.

ṭ represents the hard Semitic *t* (Arabic ط, Hebrew ט).

The ordinary *spiritus lenis* has been dispensed with generally, but is represented by ʾ (Hebrew א) in particular cases.

The Semitic ע (ʻ*ayin*) is marked by ʻ, except where custom omits it.

Long vowels in Arabic and pure-long ones in Hebrew are marked with a circumflex. Other long vowels, including tone-long ones in Hebrew, are marked ¯.

CONTENTS

PLANS AND ILLUSTRATIONS

MAPS

SAMARIA IN AHAB'S TIME

CHAPTER I

THE PALACE AND OTHER BUILDINGS

THE ancient city of Samaria, 'the head of Ephraim' (Is 7^{9}), lies immediately west of the modern village of *Sebustieh* (Greek, Sebaste), which was the new name given to the place by Herod the Great when he rebuilt it (B.C. 27) in honour of Augustus. From the seventh year of King Omri (*c.* 880 B.C.) the kings of Israel (or 'Ephraim,' as the prophets called the northern kingdom) [1] had their palace there, though during the early period of the monarchy they seem to have had a residence also at Jezreel (1 K 18^{45}, 2 K 8^{29}), in order probably to strengthen their alliance

[1] Ephraim (? 'fertile region') was in reality a city (2 Ch 13^{19}, 2 S 13^{23}), generally identified with modern *eṭ-Ṭaiyibeh*, south of Shechem, though the name was also applied to the tribe and afterwards to the northern kingdom. Mount Ephraim (הַר אֶפְרָאִים, Jos 17^{15} 19^{50}, etc.) was the designation of the western range of hills (a single compact *massif*) from Esdraelon as far south at least as Bethel, just as Mount Judah (הַר יְהוּדָה) was the name given to the whole tableland of Judah (Jos 21^{11}, where the expression is translated 'hill country of Judah'). One important difference between Mount Ephraim and Mount Judah is that the former slopes gradually to the west by uninterrupted ridges, while the latter is bordered by precipices and defiles. Hence the former was more easily attacked by enemies, and required forts at the passes.

with Phœnicia. Judging from 1 K 21¹, as generally translated, one is apt to conclude that the palace referred to in this verse, adjoining which lay Naboth's vineyard, must have been the one at Jezreel; [1] but apart from the different view presented by the LXX in the text (in both Vat. and Alex. MSS.), the fact that Naboth dwelt in Jezreel did not prevent him owning property in Samaria, and according to 21^{18} the vineyard may have been in the latter city. After Omri had built a palace here on the summit of the hill, Ahab seems to have enlarged and beautified it, and it may have been for this purpose that he coveted the neighbouring ground.

The site was a central and dominant one, worth consolidating. It was much stronger than that of Shechem, the earliest capital of the land, for Shechem, though well furnished with water and possessing sacred associations, could never be turned into a fortress, and was not fitted for defence. It was preferable also to Tirṣah, the capital of Jeroboam I., which was unsuited to a dynasty in alliance with Phœnicia, and was too open to attack by the Aramæan States on the north-east. The site even took natural precedence over that of Jerusalem, which was an awkward and barren one. The hill ('mountain of Samaria,' Am 4^1 6^1), rising as a round and isolated mass from 300 to 400 feet above the valley, could offer a stubborn resistance to the best-

[1] So Buhl, *Geogr. des Alten Palästina*, p. 204; Guérin, *Samarie*, i. p. 313; Josephus, *Antiq.* VIII. xv. 6.

organized armies.[1] We can understand the remark of Adad-idri's officers after their defeat, 'Their god is a god of the hills, therefore they were stronger than we; but let us fight against them in the plain, and surely we shall be stronger than they' (1 K 20[23]). Samaria alone of all the surrounding districts was able to cope with the invasion of Tiglath-pileser III. in 733–732 B.C., and it was only captured by Sargon II. in 722 after three years' effort. This Assyrian monarch carried off 27,000 people into captivity, and appointed an Assyrian governor over the remainder. After this the city was occupied chiefly by foreign colonists whom the Assyrian kings installed in place of the exiled Israelites, and it was refortified with a strong surrounding wall half-way down the hill and an inner wall round the summit. From this time onward to the fourth century B.C., its history is almost unknown. It was captured by Alexander the Great on his way back from Egypt in 331 B.C., when he punished the inhabitants for murdering his governor, Andromachus,[2] and settled it with Macedonian colonists.[3] It suffered

[1] For the strength of the position, see Josephus, *Antiq.* XIII. x. 2. It is possible that the name of the hill, Shômerôn (שֹׁמְרוֹן), Aramaic Shâmerên, may signify 'watch-mountain,' 'outlook' (cf. 'Wartburg'), from שָׁמַר, although a derivation from Shemer (a clan-name used as a personal name?), who is stated to have been the former owner, is given in 1 K 16[24]. If the name be from שָׁמַר, it is appropriate, for the hill commands a wide view to the west. Some 8 miles of plain are visible, then a range of low hills, and beyond them the Mediterranean, 23 miles away.

[2] Q. Curtius, iv. 5, 9, and iv. 8, 9 (ed. Lemaire).

[3] Schürer, *Hist.* Div. II. vol i. p. 123.

severely in the wars of the Diadochi, and its fortifications are said to have been overthrown by Ptolemy Lagos in his retreat from Syria before Antigonus.[1] But it seems to have survived wonderfully well through all these vicissitudes, with practically the same topographical features. About 107 B.C., however, when it was almost entirely Seleucid, it was completely demolished by John Hyrcanus, not by turning on it streams of water as some historians state, but by exposing it to the washing of the winter torrents, and breaching it so that it fell in confused ruins. 'He demolished it entirely, and brought rivulets to it to drown it, for he dug such hollows as might let the water run under it.'[2]

The recent account by the Harvard University archæologists (Professor George A. Reisner, Mr. Clarence S. Fisher, architect, and Professor David G. Lyon) of excavations on the site of this ancient capital,[3] together with comments by René Dussaud[4] and others, throws considerable light on the successive periods of occupation. One cannot study this careful and detailed account without being

[1] Diodorus Siculus, xix. 93. [2] Josephus, *Antiq.* XIII. x. 3.

[3] *Harvard Excavations at Samaria* (1908–10), two large volumes beautifully printed and illustrated (Harvard University Press, 1924: vol. i., xxxii+417 pp.; vol. ii., xxii+16 plans+90 plates). The excavations were begun in 1908 by Dr. Gottlieb Schumacher, whose work at *Tell el-Mutesellim* had already gained him world-wide reputation, and were continued by the archæologists mentioned. The long postponement of publication has been due to unforeseen circumstances. The volumes are quoted hereafter in footnotes simply as *Excavations*.

[4] 'Samarie au Temps d'Achab,' *Revue Syria*, 1925, iv. pp. 314 ff.; 1926, i. pp. 9 ff.

reminded with singular force of the glorious past of this rival to Jerusalem, the activity and military valour of its kings, the ardour of its prophets, and its final overthrow by the Assyrian armies. Before the archæologists began their work, the hill of Samaria was covered with soil under cultivation. As the result of wars, treasure searches, removal of building stones, quarrying, and agricultural labours during the last twenty centuries, the ancient Israelite and other walls, together with thousands of interesting objects, lay buried in the depths. The only vestiges of antiquity visible were some of the towers and columns of the Herodian period. It was the work of the excavators to disentangle the various strata, from the Arabic and Roman on the top, through the Seleucid and Babylonian, down to the lowest or Israelite at the bottom. This formed a difficult problem, owing to the alteration of the older strata by later buildings, and in the solution of it they had to rely largely on the types of masonry, the relative heights of floors, the objects unearthed, the nature of the debris, and other criteria. Fortunately, with their scholarship and acute discernment, they have been able to penetrate to the times of Ahab and Omri, although not many vestiges of this ancient period remain after the subsequent reconstructions, and especially after the removal of the materials to *Sebustieh* for the erection of the buildings there.[1] In dealing with the Israelite

[1] Guérin, *Samarie*, ii. p. 195.

strata, they had to exercise special care, as the building operations of the later periods tended naturally to transfer pottery and other objects from lower to higher levels. It will be agreed, however, by all readers of the report that they have succeeded remarkably well in differentiating the Israelite remains from the later ones. The result is that we have valuable documents and important information regarding the history of Israel. If Psalm 45 be taken as presenting a picture of royal life and society in the first years of the Israelite monarchy, probably as some think in the time of Ahab (*c.* 875–853 B.C.), the excavations do nothing at least to weaken such a view. They give us a picture of the grandeur of Samaria, especially in his day, with its strong walls, its palaces, its private houses built with hewn stone (Am 5^{11}), its perfect organization, its riches, and its power. Renan has said that Ahab 'equalled Solomon in mental grasp and surpassed him in military valour.'[1] Certainly, judging from the Harvard account, he seems to have developed Israelite civilization. The work of the excavators, it should be said, has likewise thrown great light on the Babylonian, Grecian, and Herodian periods. No less than 2921 photographs of objects and various details of the work were taken.

The account affords confirmation of the Biblical fact (1 K 16^{24}) that the site had no buildings on it and was probably little inhabited before the time

[1] *Histoire du peuple d'Israël,* ii. p. 301.

of Omri (*c.* 887–875 B.C.). The Israelite buildings were found to rest on the ancient rock-surface beneath, to which the excavations have been pushed. This surface at its highest area (the Omri scarp) bears the channels and cup-marks common on rock all over Palestine, as well as a few cuttings for trough presses and jar sockets of various types.[1] The surface must have been in this bare condition, covered to the top with soil and rock, when Omri bought the hill for two shekels of silver,[2] and erected his palace there. 'It is clear,' says Professor Reisner, 'that the rock was at least partly bare when the palace was begun, and, as far as the present excavations have extended, it was everywhere stripped for quarrying and building.'[3] No ceramic remains or traces of dwellings previous to Omri's date can be found: the only vestiges of occupation beyond the iron age belong to the neolithic period. The body of the hill is penetrated by a number of caves, apparently natural, but more or less modified by the Israelites and their successors (the soft limestone of which the hill is made offered no special difficulties). These cannot compare in size and number with those discovered in other parts of

[1] The presses consisted of broad beds of rock, frequently circular, surrounded by deep narrow channels which collected the liquid (from olives or grapes). From these channels, surface conduits led to collecting bowls (cf. Macalister, *Excavation of Gezer*, ii. pp. 48 ff.). The sockets were for holding the pointed oil and wine jars characteristic of the period.

[2] For the purchase, cf. the case of David, 2 S 24[21ff.].

[3] *Excavations*, i. p. 60.

Palestine, such as at Mareshah, Gezer, and Megiddo, and there are no primitive scratchings of animal figures in them. Some of them have rude steps cut down into them, and were occupied even as late as the Roman period, but fragments of Israelite pottery and other objects have been found in them. They remind us of the Biblical statement that, at the time of Jezebel's persecution of Yahweh's prophets, Obadiah took a hundred of these and 'hid them by fifty in a cave' (1 K 18^4).

Only one gate into the town is mentioned in the Old Testament. In ancient times the number of gates into a town was kept as low as possible—Jericho seems to have had only one—so that it might be difficult for an enemy to enter. The gate of Samaria has been found on the west, with traces of primitive fortification. As the high ground on which the Israelite town stood is isolated on all sides except the east, where it is connected with the hill by a low narrow saddle, it is evident that the position of the gate was well chosen to make access difficult in a hostile attack, for an enemy could only approach with any facility along the saddle, and would thus be forced—until at least the battering-ram was perfected—to proceed round the whole wall before finding an entrance. The fortification at the gate consisted in a square tower or citadel, measuring 57·41 feet by 44·29 feet, of solid, well-built masonry, which dates according to Fisher from the time of Omri. The tower enabled the defenders to make the gate a death-trap to any attacking party, for the latter would be confined

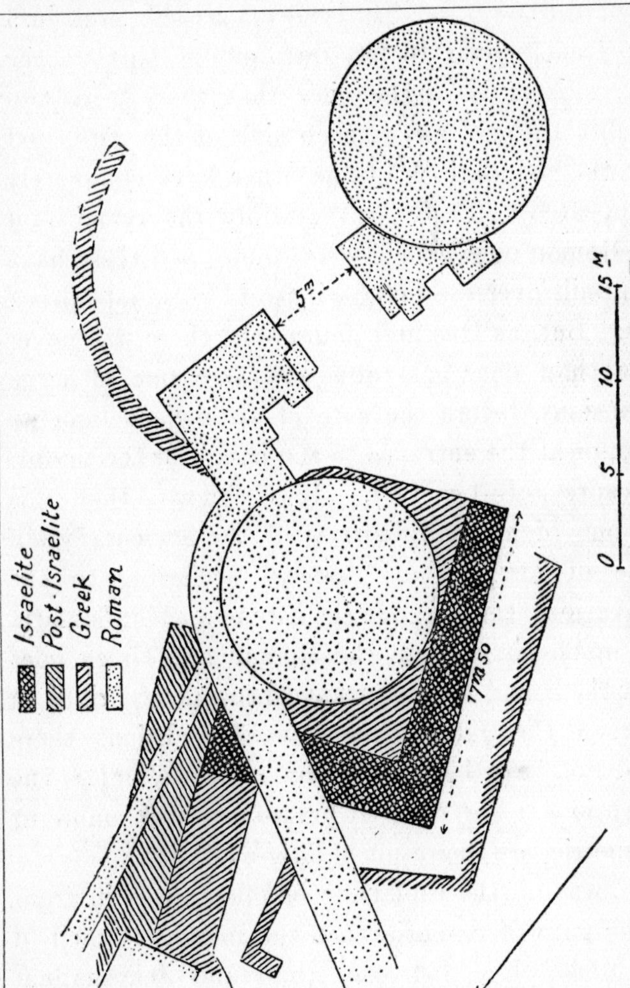

The Successive States of the Gate of the Town
(From *Excavations*, ii. pl. 10)

within a narrow space, exposed to ceaseless attack overhead. It made defence far superior to attack, and without a siege-train such a fort could only be reduced by stratagem or by starvation. The bottom of the tower has been unearthed, sunk in a deep trench (over 16 feet deep at one part) in the rock. Fisher is of the view that there were two Israelite towers, one at each side of the gate, and that the foundations of the other have completely disappeared.[1] There are certainly the remains of two Roman ones, which were round, and these have been built over the foundations of two square Greek ones. But, as Dussaud points out, there was never more than one, generally a square one of large dimensions, before the gate of an ancient Israelite town, or at the entrance to the palace or the temple enclosure (cf. Gn 11^4). It is known that this was one of the peculiarities of the ancient Syrian mode of fortification. Indeed, according to the excavations, the tower at the gate of ancient Samaria was much larger than the Roman and Greek ones unearthed, and seems to have been placed right in front of the gate. Under such conditions there could not have been room for a second, unless the dimensions were reduced. Two towers, round or symmetric, are the result of later evolution.[2]

It was on the esplanade or open space in front of the gate of Samaria that the famous council of war took place between Ahab and Jehoshaphat

[1] *Excavations*, i. p. 120.

[2] This view is controverted by Vincent (*Revue biblique*, Oct. 1926, pp. 631 f.), but he fails to give any satisfactory evidence against it.

when they decided to attack Ramoth-Gilead in spite of Micaiah's warning. Here too the public market was held to which people round about brought their wheat, barley, and other produce (2 K 7[1]), and here justice was administered and punishment meted out. The gate of an Israelite city was the natural centre of life, where meetings

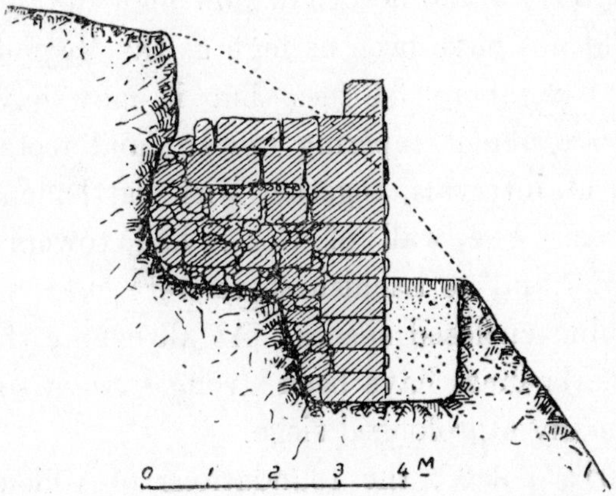

SECTION OF THE SOUTH WALL OF THE TOWN
(From *Excavations*, i. p. 121)

were held and business transactions carried through, and where the daily news was discussed.

The ancient defensive wall of the town, dating it is thought from Omri's and Ahab's time, must have been of massive construction. It has been unearthed only in two places—at the western gate, and at one point towards the south where it is found to be about 10 feet thick with bosses on all the outer stones. The ground slopes down considerably on the outside of the wall here, and to prevent the front of the latter from slipping down the cliff it has been placed over 3 feet back from the verge, and its foundations have been sunk about 6 feet deep into the rocky bottom. In this way the building of a formidable supporting glacis, such as existed at Megiddo, was avoided. Unfortunately, we do not know how high the wall was. It could not have been as high as the Megiddo one, which was about 34 feet, but it may have had buttresses like it tapering upward and rectangular towers at intervals, together with battlements and palisades. The wall of Gezer had towers every 30 yards, and at Lachish there were even bastions containing enclosed spaces. At all events the wall of Samaria must have been strong enough to withstand many a prolonged siege.

Omri's palace, the foundations of which have been excavated to the solid rock cut to receive them, lies on the ancient summit of the hill, on an artificially faced pinnacle or platform, just east of the apparent modern summit. There is, of course, no absolute proof that this building was a palace or part of a palace: it may have been a temple. But the plan, situation, size, and strength all go to show that it was probably the royal dwelling, and being the earliest building on the summit (the primary building site) the excavators have attributed it to Omri. It has thick, heavy walls, and according to the plan very common in eastern countries is composed of various halls abutting on open courts. Its walls are

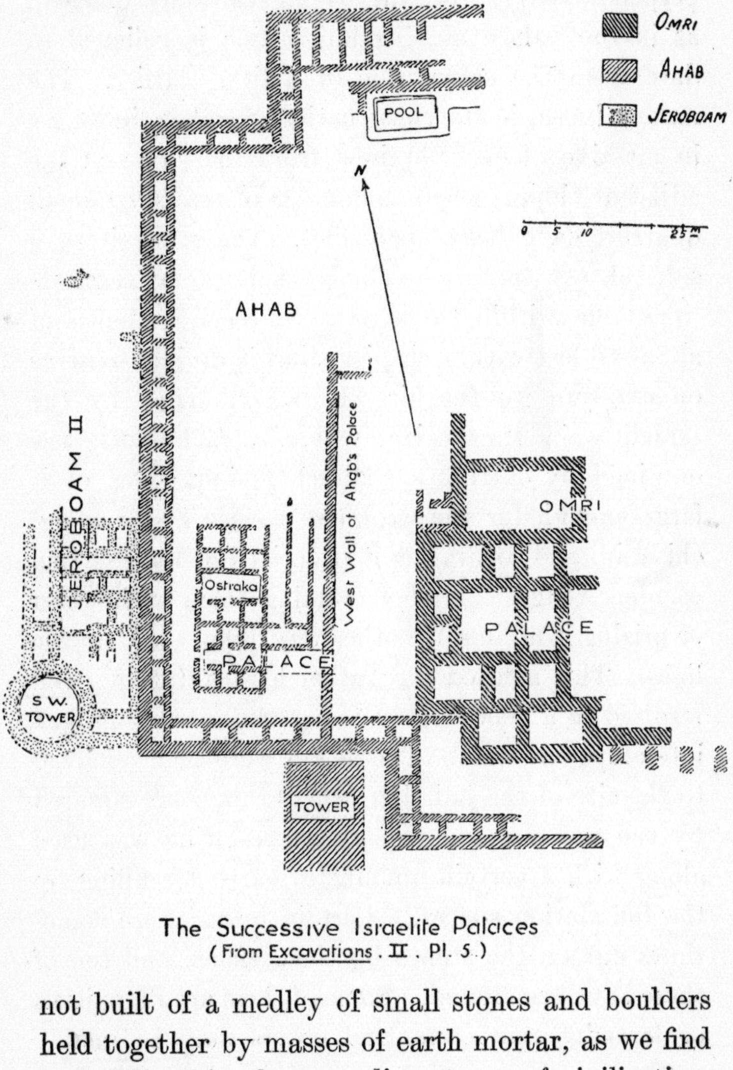

The Successive Israelite Palaces
(From Excavations. II. Pl. 5.)

not built of a medley of small stones and boulders held together by masses of earth mortar, as we find in buildings in the preceding stages of civilization, but there is an intelligent arrangement of large dressed stones, fitted and jointed horizontally and perpendicularly, with the edging carefully finished, as in the palace at Megiddo, which is believed to date from the same time or a little earlier. The material used in the construction is yellow limestone in massive blocks, obtained from the site and the adjacent slopes, where a number of scattered small quarries have been uncovered. The stone is of a soft, cheesy texture—so soft that the excavators were able within three days to reach a depth of about 10 feet with their picks, but it rapidly hardens on exposure to the air. It was quarried by the Israelites in the ancient way, *i.e.* each block was obtained by cutting a channel on four sides of it large enough for the workman to use his arm and chisel in, and separating it from its bed by inserting wooden wedges and then wetting them with water or prizing it up in some other way along the cleavage lines. This method was rather a wasteful one, and resulted in a good deal of the stratum being broken into chips and dust. The blocks were then removed to the site of the building, where they were squared by the masons, and any debris resulting was used along with a certain amount of earth for filling up the foundation spaces.[1] Certain marks were sometimes cut on the stones by the masons, and ten of these have been found. Some of them are Phœnician or Israelite characters, and others may be merely

[1] *Excavations*, i. p. 37.

key marks. Many of the exterior stones of Omri's palace, below ground, have a heavy, rough boss with a marginal dressing (done with a broad adze) on the edges, like the rusticated work of the Pitti

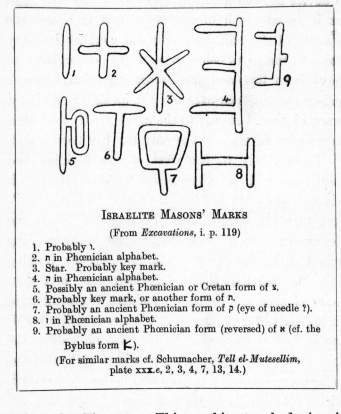

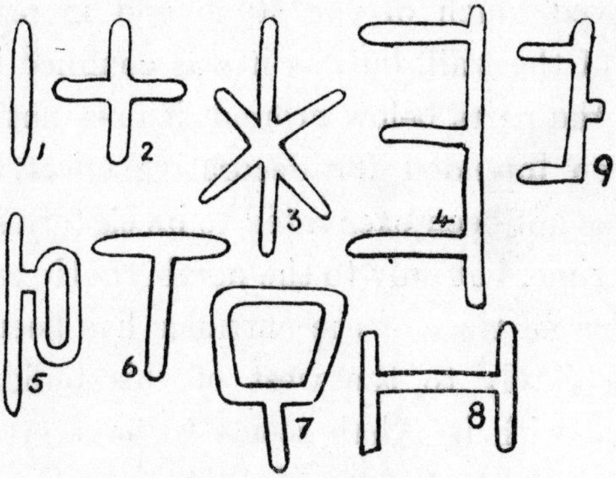

ISRAELITE MASONS' MARKS

(From *Excavations*, i. p. 119)

1. Probably ו.
2. ח in Phœnician alphabet.
3. Star. Probably key mark.
4. ה in Phœnician alphabet.
5. Possibly an ancient Phœnician or Cretan form of צ.
6. Probably key mark, or another form of ח.
7. Probably an ancient Phœnician form of ק (eye of needle ?).
8. ז in Phœnician alphabet.
9. Probably an ancient Phœnician form (reversed) of א (cf. the Byblus form K).

(For similar marks cf. Schumacher, *Tell el-Mutesellim*, plate xxx.*e*, 2, 3, 4, 7, 13, 14.)

Palace in Florence. This architectural device is found more regularly under Ahab, and was common for many ages in Syria and Palestine. It has been found in the walls at *Ṣafi*, *Zakariyeh*, and *Tell el-Ḥesy*, assigned by scholars to Rehoboam (*c.* 937 B.C.), where the masonry shows large bosses and a margin varying from 2 to 4 inches in breadth. It appears also in the walls at *Es-Salt* (Penuel ?), which are believed to date from Ahab's time or earlier.[1] Such a device showed a certain amount of care and skill, as it saved much of the stone and increased the solidity of the wall, but, as it was confined in many cases to the parts below ground, it does not seem to have been intended for decorative effect. Omri's palace has not been excavated to its eastern limit for want of time, but only to the north, south, and west, and so far no trace of the entrance has been found.

Immediately to the west of this building and connected with it, Ahab seems to have erected his 'ivory palace' (1 K 22^{39}, cf. Ps 45^{8}), making Omri's structure the basis of it. There is, of course, no definite proof that this second portion of the building was Ahab's palace, but it was probably his, judging from the fact that it is a large structure, second in point of time, and bears a considerable resemblance in the character of its masonry to an Israelite building at *Tell el-Mutesellim*.[2] This second palace, the foundations of which were also laid in rock cuttings, is far more extensive in plan and better constructed. Fisher thinks it bears a resemblance to the Assyrian palaces, but the outside arrangement forbids this. A typical Assyrian palace is that of Sargon II. at Dur-Sharrukin (*Khorsabâd*), consisting of a huge

[1] *Palestine Exploration Fund Quarterly Statement*, April 1928, p. 98.
[2] Schumacher, *Tell el-Mutesellim*, i. p. 91.

walled square, with numerous buildings and inner courts, including a *ziggurat* and other temples. Ahab's was different: its architecture was probably fostered by Tyrian influence. David had to send to King Hiram of Tyre for masons and carpenters to build his palace, and Solomon found it necessary to employ Phœnician skill in the construction of his spacious buildings. The Phœnicians were well known as expert workmen in hewn stone. They had to accustom themselves to stonework, for they occupied a rocky coast where brick was less obtainable, and a wet coast where stone was more necessary. They seem to have learned the mason trade from outside, probably from Crete, for peculiar masons' marks have enabled scholars to trace the art back to that island.[1] Ahab accordingly fell back doubtless on Phœnician help, and all the more readily because of his alliance with Tyre. The palace is composed of three parts: first, the palace properly so called; then a vast outer court, 104 yards long, enclosed by a heavy retaining wall over 6 feet thick, around which was a series of small rooms, serving no doubt as domestic offices, chariot-houses, and stables; and lastly, a strong rectangular tower (41 feet by 52·50 feet) outside this court, in an angle at the south-west corner, where Fisher thinks it probably guarded one of the entrances to the palace, perhaps a kind of postern or small gateway. For the con-

[1] Bertholet, *History of Hebrew Civilization*, English ed., p. 208, with references there.

2

struction of the buildings large blocks of yellow limestone, smoothly dressed, were used, and as these must have been of lighter shade when the palace was erected, this fact has led Reisner to conclude that herein lies the origin of the term 'ivory palace.'[1] But this term could hardly be explained in such a way, unless the stone were coated with lime or whitewash. This, of course, may have been the case, for whitewash is frequently mentioned in connection with buildings (cf. Ezk 13^10. 12. 14 22^28). It produced a dazzling white colour, in contrast with the blue of the sky. The term 'ivory,' however, was applied rather to houses the rooms of which were panelled or decorated with this substance (cf. Am 3^15), as many rooms still are in Damascus and other cities of the East. The Egyptian and Babylonian monuments refer to the widespread trade in ivory, and Ahab must have had no difficulty in securing sufficient quantities of this material from Tyre, which was the principal centre of the trade (Ezk 27^6. 15). An ivory box found at Enkomi in Cyprus, picturing a Syrian or Phœnician chariot, dates from this epoch.[2] In the courtyard of Ahab's palace the excavators discovered an ivory handle (mirror handle ?) carved in the form of a winged Uræus wearing the Egyptian crown, and an ivory dagger handle with the end shaped in the form

[1] *Excavations*, i. p. 61.
[2] Dussaud, *Civilizations pré-helléniques*, 2e éd., fig. 199.

of a snarling lion's head; and in the early debris elsewhere they found fragments of ivory, including an object shaped like an Egyptian breast pendant, in the form of a Bes-head, with ornamental collar.[1] It was not inappropriate that a king who could cope with the Aramæans of Damascus, and whose power extended as far as Moab and was recognized by Phœnicia and Judah, should build himself a luxurious 'ivory' palace befitting the civilization of the times. The King of Damascus had an ivory bed (cf. Am 6^4, where such beds are mentioned) and a massive ivory throne which Adad-nirari III. carried off as booty,[2] and Solomon possessed an ivory throne overlaid with gold (1 K 10^{18}).

Unfortunately, as none of the superstructure of the palace remains, it is impossible to form any idea of the height. But there must have been upper rooms (עֲלִיָּה), and if so, chimneys, for it is known that the larger houses had 'smoke-holes' (Hos 13^3), and it is difficult to understand how smoke could escape otherwise in two-storied buildings. The

[1] Numerous figures of the Egyptian god Bes or Ptah-Seker (probably the original of the Satyr or 'Silen' of the Greek vase-painters) in stone and earthenware have been unearthed in Palestine (cf. *P.E.F. Quarterly Statement*, April 1928, p. 85). He is represented as a misshapen dwarf-god, with legs too short, abdomen prominent, arms bent, chin bearded, tongue hanging out, and face grinning. It is rather difficult to understand the meaning of such figures, which had an enormous vogue in western Asia. They may have been intended either in a comical sense to provoke laughter or in some other sense as mascots to drive away demons (cf. Erman, *Die Aegyptische Religion* (1905), p. 78). A clay mould has been found at Gezer for manufacturing these images.

[2] Dhorme, *Les Pays bibliques et l'Assyrie*, p. 28.

upper room, from which King Ahaziah, son and successor of Ahab, fell (2 K 1^{2}), seems to have been a belvedere, probably upon a turret-like annexe or above the flat roof at one corner, and he may have been leaning on the lattice or balustrade (שְׂבָכָה) when this gave way and he fell through it (cf. Dt 22^{8}). No doubt the palace, like every large dwelling, had both winter and summer quarters (cf. Jer 36^{22}, Am 3^{15}), an arrangement still common in Palestine ('*beit shatawy*' and '*beit seify*'). Either the interior and more sheltered rooms would form the winter house and the exterior and airy ones the summer one, or, what was more probable in the case of two-storied dwellings, the lower rooms would be used in winter and the upper ones in summer (cf. Jg 3^{20}, 'upper chamber of cooling'), as in the Lebanon at the present day. In the winter quarters there would probably be a stove, or at least a brazier, for protection against the cold (cf. Jehoiachim's, Jer 36^{22}). Some of these braziers were beautifully ornamented articles. One found at Taanach was something like an altar, about 3 feet high, decorated with cherub heads, and with Babylonian and Cyprian subjects in relief.[1]

One of the most interesting parts of the palace laid bare is the tower (*armôn*, אַרְמוֹן, 2 K 15^{25}; cf. Tirṣah, 1 K 16^{18}) in front of the entrance, in which the royal guard generally lived so as to be

[1] Sellin, *Tell Ta'annek*, i. pp. 76, 109; Thiersch, in *Archäologischer Anzeiger* (1909), p. 404; Bertholet, *History of Hebrew Civilization*, English ed., p. 170.

near the palace without being inside it. It was in this very tower that King Pekahiah was assassinated by his chief officer, Pekah (2 K 15[25]). In the days before Omri, when Tirṣah was the capital of Israel, the royal palace there also possessed a protective tower or *armôn* (1 K 16[18]), and when Omri attacked the town Zimri fled to this place of defence, set fire to it, and perished in the flames. Dussaud may be right in concluding that this fire was one of the reasons which, at a time when the Assyrian menace was becoming threatening, led Omri to found another capital, and it is not improbable that the *armôn* at Samaria, ascribed by the excavators to Ahab, may date from Omri's reign, especially as it is only about 10 yards from the latter's palace.

A peculiar feature of the inner part of Ahab's palace is a room, from which a trench or long cut in the rock, 2 feet 7 inches deep, roofed with flat stones so as to form a tunnel, leads into a square chamber under a court of Omri's palace.[1] This underground chamber has a round hole cut in the roof of it, but whether the hole was originally there or was made later is unknown. Its purpose may have been to admit light from above. The chamber has a width of 13·50 feet by 19·50 feet, and an average height of about 12 feet, and may have been originally one of the numerous caves found in the hill. It lies under the earliest Greek walls, and was at first thought to be an ordinary cistern, but from the

[1] *Excavations*, i. pp. 61, 95.

carefully constructed tunnel it seems to have served some other purpose, perhaps a palace treasure chamber, as Reisner suggests, or probably a prison for defaulters in the royal service. Was it here that Micaiah the prophet was imprisoned for his unwelcome message to Ahab (1 K 22^{27})? The chamber was found to be full of debris of the post-exilic period, in which were a large number of Greek and Palestinian potsherds from inscribed jars (of date 600–400 B.C.), including eight with inscriptions in characters resembling the middle Aramaic of the Persian period.[1] These were written in black ink, but unfortunately the lettering has long since grown faded owing to the damp. There were also three bone spatulæ or styli, a bronze cosmetic spoon, a bronze chisel, an iron point, a carved bone, and over a hundred dressed or split bones of domestic animals, apparently kitchen debris.

Within the great courtyard of Ahab's palace, near the southern extremity of it, there are the remains of a fairly large building (82 feet by 36 feet), containing eighteen roughly built square rooms, in three groups of six each, opening off corridors. This has apparently been the residence of the royal stewards or at least a magazine or storehouse for oil and wine brought to the palace as revenue, as the *ostraka* mentioning these products were found in it. We are reminded of the storehouses in

[1] Cf. Lidzbarski, *Handbuch der Nord-semitischen Epigraphik*, II. Teil, pl. xlv. cols. 5–9.

Jerusalem that Hezekiah built in which to store the consignments of grain, wine, and oil which came to the capital (2 Ch 32[28]). This building, which has been called the '*ostraka* house,' was perhaps the place that Ben-hadad II. (Adad-idri) was anxious to search in addition to Ahab's palace (1 K 20[6]). At the north end of the courtyard is a cemented pool or reservoir for water (32·50 feet by 17 feet, but sometime later the size was lessened), about 20 inches deeper at one end than the other. The bottom and sides have at least two layers of greyish cement (mixed with wood ashes) as hard as the rock beneath. This pond must have served for watering the horses and cleaning the chariots. We cannot help recalling the historic scene when Ahab, after being mortally wounded at the attack on Ramoth-Gilead, bled to death in his chariot, and his servants washed it along with his armour in the 'pool of Samaria' (1 K 22[38]).[1]

After Ahab's death, other buildings with even better masonry were added immediately beyond the courtyard on the west side. These include a great circular defensive tower (diameter about 32 feet inside), with walls over 7 feet thick, and are attributed tentatively by the excavators to Jeroboam II. (*c.* 785 ?). Altogether, from Omri's time onward, there must have been almost constant building going on in Samaria, especially in connection with the royal dwellings and precincts. It is not im-

[1] According to most critics this verse is an interpolation intended as a fulfilment to the prediction in 21[19].

probable that this involved a large amount of forced service, for only in this way could such work have been possible. In Judah, at least, bodies of forced labourers (מַס) were utilized for public services under the kings. They seem to have been constituted by David, who appointed Adoram as master over them (2 S 20^{24}).[1] Large gangs of such workmen were employed by Solomon in the erection of the temple and other buildings. These included not only Israelites drawn by levy from the people (1 K 5^{13} 9^{15}), but vassal Canaanites (1 K 9^{21}, 2 Ch 8^{8}; cf. Dt 20^{11}, Jos 16^{10}, etc.). Probably the former were not as harshly treated as the latter, but their yoke was undoubtedly grievous (1 K 12^{4}). In the northern kingdom, a similar *corvée* no doubt existed. Ahab's 'ivory' palace and 'all the cities which he built' (1 K 22^{39}) must have required considerable bodies of quarrymen, burden-bearers, builders, and other labourers, working under taskmasters. Large numbers of them must have been bondmen in all but name, for purposes which had little connection with their own welfare. In this respect the purple of Ahab and the other rulers of the northern kingdom, like the imperial robes of Solomon, may have had a very seamy side, and considerable hardship and misery may have existed under the luxury and splendour they enjoyed.

[1] The rendering of מַס by 'tribute,' as in this and other texts, is incorrect and misleading. Its meaning is collective: 'forced labourers,' 'labour-gang.' In later times, it came to have a somewhat concrete sense, 'forced service,' 'serfdom,' and in Est 10^{1} it possibly means 'forced payment.'

CHAPTER II

ISRAELITE ART

It is probably true, as Bertholet says, that 'Palestine offered no encouragement to its inhabitants in respect of art.'[1] Bare and unwooded, only cultivated here and there, with few flowers and little grass except in spring, and vegetation dead in autumn and winter, the country presented what Benzinger has called 'a drab picture, uninteresting and wearisome to look upon.'[2] The Canaanites, Israelites, and other inhabitants had thus little opportunity of learning the meaning of beauty. In the case of the Israelites, too, the imitation of all living forms was forbidden (Ex 20^4), and although images certainly existed among them, they were only tolerated on sufferance. This was a bar to any development of sculpture or plastic art, and it is on this account probably that no pieces of Israelite sculpture of any sort have been discovered in Samaria. In the various forms of art, æsthetic and mechanical, and in representations, the Israelites were behind other nations. One could hardly expect, indeed,

[1] *History of Hebrew Civilization*, English ed., p. 29.
[2] *Hebräische Archäologie* (1907), p. 19.

to find the same power of art anywhere in Palestine as in the neighbouring land of Egypt.

At the same time, it cannot be said that none worthy of the name existed. We know that the inhabitants could make fine-looking chariots, and bronze weapons of an artistic type. The description of the booty captured by Thutmose III. at Megiddo (*c.* 1500 B.C.) shows that at that early period they possessed various products of an artistic culture. Both from Canaanite and Israelite debris, large quantities of pottery and clay figures have been unearthed in recent years, and though these have none of the beauty of the Egyptian glazed ceramic, they show a certain amount of artistic skill. Pottery began in Palestine as far back as the Neolithic age, when it was made entirely by hand. Some of the better specimens still bear the marks of the fingers. When ornamentation was attempted, it consisted generally of mere lines, sometimes undulating, but often in trellis-form, ladder-form, or chessboard arrangement. These lines were generally scratched in the smooth clay with the help of a piece of flint or bone well pointed or toothed like a fine saw, but sometimes they were laid on with coarse red colour over a yellowish-white ground. Later on, in the earliest historic period (down to 1600 B.C.), pottery work began to be an art owing largely to Babylonian, Egyptian, and other foreign influences, and the vessels took on some beauty of form and surface. The outside became glossier, either by smoothing it with the hands or polishing it with a sharp tool. The simple line ornamentation of the Neolithic age was not yet entirely given up, but there began to be designs in colour, with patterns from nature, such as plants and trees (*e.g.* the tree of life) and animals (particularly birds, fishes, and ibexes), and there were efforts to make vessels or parts of vessels in the shape of animals (*e.g.* a horse-head, with bridle). About 1600 B.C. the potter's art entered on a stage of great advance. The next few centuries were the golden age of Palestinian ceramics. This was due to two causes, one of which was the introduction into Palestine of the potter's wheel (though this at first was only employed in a few places and on rare occasions), and the other was the influence of the West, which now began to make itself felt and to fill Palestine with its wares. The imitation of western ceramics and of Mycenæan art began, and although the productions were coarser and more limited than the models, yet undoubted progress was made. The jars began to have a more graceful neck and a more slender outline, and to have imitations on them of birds, gazelles, imaginary quadrupeds, and other natural objects, including even creatures of polyparian shape. By the time the Israelites took possession of the land, the potter's art was widespread. The potter had learned to use both his hands and his feet—his hands to shape the clay, and his feet to knead it (Is 41[25]) and drive the wheel (Sir 38[29]). He had the benefit too of the imported

Greek, or rather Cyprian, wares, which were beginning to come into Palestine in increasing numbers through the Phœnician ports, and which were generally coated with yellow-brown enamel and had dark concentric rings painted over them. These wares were largely sub-Mycenæan, *i.e.* they represented Mediterranean (Ægean and Mycenæan) influences, which still survived through the intermediary of Cyprus and of the Asiatic littoral. The spread of them was assisted by the conquest and domination of the Philistines. The Israelites set themselves to imitate these wares, but their materials were naturally coarser and the shapes not so artistic. Indeed, the inspiration of the potter's art in Palestine was waning, and by the time of Ahab we witness a decline both in technique and ornamentation. The clay used was less pure, the paste less fine, the curves less elegant, and the forms less varied.[1]

This is borne out by the Israelite pottery, of date 900–700 B.C., unearthed at Samaria. It consists of fragments found in the floor debris of the Ahab courtyard (where the *ostraka* were found) and the ground underneath. It comprises vessels employed in daily life for cooking, eating, and drinking, and for storing grain, milk, honey, water, wine, oil, and other things ; but it includes also some finer fabrics, such as vases and ornamental vessels. Most of it is

[1] Cf. Vincent, 'Céramique de la Palestine,' in *Union Académique internationale*, p. 19: 'Si le décor simple garde encore quelque caractère, l'ornementation peinte s'atrophie dans la sécheresse et la banalité d'un style géométrique dénué de toute inspiration.'

ordinary wheel-made pottery, of brown ware burning red when well baked, or grey ware burning drab or pink when well baked, and the bowls and jugs of this type have a thick red hæmatite coating. Much of it, however, is of a better quality, consisting of brown-red ware, with pebble-burnished, red hæmatite wash. Practically all this pottery belonging to the Israelite age accords with what we have said above. It shows no great æsthetic ideal, but generally speaking simply an effort to serve the common uses of everyday life. It is easily distinguished from that of the next period (the Babylonio-Grecian), which consists largely of Greek wares of black-figured, red-figured, and white-ground fabrics. Although about a thousand handles of wine-jars were found belonging to the Hellenistic and later periods, stamped with the makers' marks, only two Israelite ones were found, the one being incised with a cross (possibly the letter ת in Phœnician), and the other with a mark which may represent ה in Phœnician. A pottery mould, of coarse black-brown ware, with a red coating, was also found in Israelite surroundings.

Among other interesting things discovered in the excavations are lamps, which, like all household utensils of potter's manufacture, have been unearthed in abundance. Some of these are whole, some broken, and almost all of them have wick-blackened spouts. At least ten have been found in Israelite and Babylonio-Grecian debris. These are all open (or saucer) lamps, except one of high form and fine drab ware which is half-closed, and all of them have one or more spouts (two of them, probably Babylonio-Grecian, have seven spouts). This style of lamp, the rim of which was pinched together at one or more places for the wick to pass through, is of Phœnician origin, and is found in the tombs and

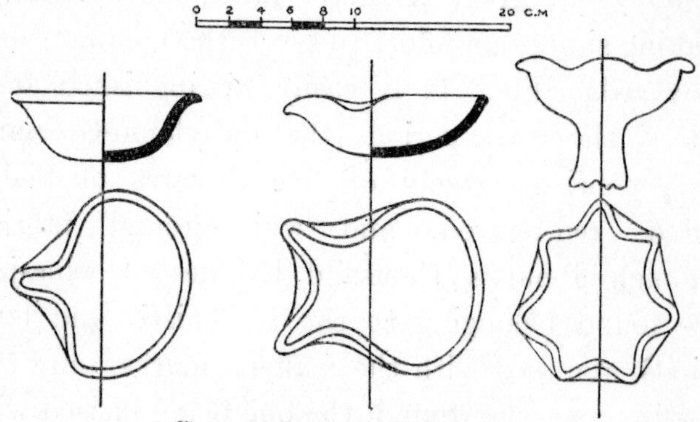

Saucer Lamps. Scale, 1 : 4
(From *Excavations*, i. p. 318)

ruins of the oldest Phœnician towns. It shows a distinct advance as compared with earlier times, when the lamp, as described by Herodotus (ii. 62), was a simple bowl or plate, with the wick floating on top of the oil. It falls, however, much behind the later high closed type of Greek manufacture, or the moulded type made in two halves, top and bottom, and stuck together before glazing.

The excavators found in the Israelite debris some

slabs and splinters of blue glass (raw material), as well as a piece of variegated (sometimes known as 'Phœnician') glass having deep blue body with white and yellow bands. These fragments of glass were no doubt imported from Phœnicia, although the Phœnicians were not the inventors of glass, as Pliny asserts.[1] The honour of its discovery must be accorded to Egypt as far back probably as the first Theban empire. The Phœnicians, however, copying the Egyptians, manufactured many fine specimens of glass ornamentation, beautifully coloured, which made Tyre and Sidon famous. Some of these must have found their way into Samaria and other Israelite districts. Blue glass, especially, was popular, and the Israelites may have ground it into a fine powder and made this into a blue pigment or paste, as was done in Egypt from the Old Empire down to Roman times.[2] Often it was made into beads and pendants, and it was also regarded as a protection against evil spirits, as it is in Palestine at the present day against the evil eye.[3]

The only metal objects found in undisturbed Israelite ground were iron arrow-heads (one with the print of the wooden shaft on the haft). Many bronze and iron objects, however, were found in mixed debris, and it is possible that some at least

[1] *Nat. Hist.* xxvi. 191.
[2] Reisner, in *Excavations*, i. p. 344.
[3] Cf. L. Bauer, *Volksleben im Lande der Bibel* (1903), p. 199.

of these may have been Israelite. The transition from bronze to iron seems to have occurred about the thirteenth or fourteenth century B.C. Two knives have been found in Palestine which go back to about 1350, the earliest known manufactured iron that can be dated.[1] But from what quarter the metal was first introduced into the land is unknown. One thing is certain, that the raw material was entirely lacking there. The introduction of iron has been connected by some scholars with the extensive and continuous invasion of people from the West, who are believed to have brought the knowledge of it from the iron-working tribes of Asia Minor, though other scholars connect it with the Hittites or Phœnicians or Arabians or the smith-tribe of Kenites.[2] It appears to have been used by the native Canaanites for their weapons and war-chariots as early as the twelfth century at least. In the papyrus Anastasi IV., belonging to the first year of Seti II. (1214–1210 B.C.), three neighbouring cities in the Kishon plain are mentioned as centres for the export of war-chariots and their parts, and there is little doubt that, though such chariots were built of wood (cf. Jos 11^{9}, 'burned their chariots'), they were plated or strengthened with iron (cf. Jos 17$^{16. 18}$, Jg 1^{19} 4$^{3. 13}$, which refer to the same district). The excavators at *Tell el-Mutesellim* (Megiddo) unearthed a smithy belong-

[1] *P.E.F. Quarterly Statement*, July 1927, p. 137.
[2] Cf. Bertholet, *History of Hebrew Civilization*, English ed., p. 91.

ing apparently to this early period, with iron dross and pieces of brown clay iron ore.[1] Flinders Petrie, in his excavations at Gerar, at the level of about 1200 B.C., found evidences of ironwork furnaces, and discovered some large hoes, a plough point, an adze, and a pick weighing seven pounds.[2] The metal, however, does not appear to have come into wide use in Palestine till about 1000 B.C., when smithies began to produce iron weapons and tools of all sorts (cf. Dt 19^{5} 27^{5}, 2 K 6^{5}, Jer 17^{1}). From this time onwards the importance of ironwork increased to such an extent that the Philistines, in order to prevent the Israelites from making swords or spears, considered it wisest to deport the Hebrew smiths from the country (1 S 13^{19}; cf. 2 K 24^{14}). The fact that only iron arrow-heads have been found in Samaria in purely Israelite debris does not signify that iron tools and weapons were not in use: it only means that the succeeding generations removed them for their own use. Bronze still continued long after Ahab's reign, and indeed did not reach its highest point in Samaria till the Hellenistic period (300–100 B.C.).

Among other objects discovered in Israelite debris were large bowls of slate, or of black and white diorite (some of the latter being translucent), though it is possible, according to Reisner, that some of these bowls may belong to the Babylonio-Grecian

[1] Schumacher, *Tell el-Mutesellim*, i. pp. 130 ff.

[2] *P.E.F. Quarterly Statement*, July 1927, p. 137.

period;[1] a large number of small whorl-shaped objects of dark grey soapstone, black slate, white limestone, bone, glass, or pottery, varied in form and size, and with a narrow hole, supposed by Reisner to be spinning whorls, but by Macalister to be buttons which were fastened with a knotted string;[2] some cowries, including one with the top cut off to form a bead, after the Egyptian manner; flat bone spatulæ or styli, rounded at one end and sharpened at the other, and supposed to be either for writing on wax or clay (as Macalister thinks),[3] or for use in one of the common household industries (as Reisner suggests); amulets and scarabs, including an Egyptian gold scarab ring; club-shaped pendants of bone, ornamented with dotted circles; a cylindrical weight made of clay and pierced for suspension; a conical pestle, in shape like a truncated pyramid; and crude figurines of females with tight-fitting robes, including one holding a tambourine on her left arm, and beating it with her right hand. There were also a number of flints found (single or double edged, and some of them serrated), and stone implements, both evidently in use in the Israelite period long after the introduction of metal, which was scarce in Palestine in those early times. Some of these, of course, may date from before the occupation of the ground by the Israelites, for numerous hewn flints, pointing back to the oldest period of the

[1] *Excavations*, i. p. 335.

[2] Cf. Macalister, *Gezer*, ii. p. 91.

[3] Cf. *op. cit.* p. 274.

Palæolithic age, have been dug up in various parts of Palestine.[1] Many of these objects which we have mentioned were not confined exclusively to the Israelite debris, but were also found in some or other of the later periods. Several things that one would expect in Israelite surroundings have not been found, but, as we said in the case of iron, this does not imply that these things were non-existent among the Israelites. It only means that succeeding people took them, or that thieves, robbers, and covetous excavators in later times lighted on them and removed them.

Mention deserves to be made of two cuneiform inscriptions apparently dating from Israelite times. The one is a fragment of a letter tablet of baked clay, containing five lines of writing (referring to the delivery of some oxen and sheep) and half the impression of an Israelite seal. The other is a beautifully cut Assyrian letter-seal of baked clay, with the name of the addressee in cuneiform (unfortunately the middle of the name is broken), and with string holes for attachment to a letter or package. As there must have been considerable intercourse in Omri's and Ahab's time between Israel and Babylonia, both commercially and politically, there may have been merchants and scribes in Samaria who were well acquainted with cuneiform writing.

[1] Cf. Blanckenhorn, *Zeitschrift für Ethnologie*, xxxvii. (1905), pp. 447 ff.; *Zeitschrift des Deutschen Palästina-Vereins*, xxxv. (1902), pp. 134 ff.

Business with the eastern lands could hardly be conducted with the Phœnician alphabet, although it must have been known to some extent in Babylonia by this time. The East could only be properly reached at this time through the cuneiform.

CHAPTER III

THE OSTRAKA

THE chief interest of the excavations lies in the *ostraka* or potsherds, sixty-three of which contain Hebrew writing fairly legible. These were discovered in the storehouse already referred to (p. 22), in the lowest part of the debris. The writing is beautifully traced by means of a reed pen, and with wonderful regularity. The ink has stood well the test of time and climate, and in the majority of cases the letters are easily decipherable.

This method of writing with pen and ink was introduced into Palestine from Egypt several centuries before Ahab, along with the so-called Phœnician alphabet. Previously the other method, which belonged to the Tigris-Euphrates region and was more adapted for cuneiform signs, had been the only one in general use. This consisted of incisions or impressions made on clay tablets or some other plastic surface by means of a stylus. On the introduction, however, of the pen-and-ink method, it largely displaced the other, and was carried far and wide by Aramæan traders. In the sculptures of the Assyrian empire (such as the reliefs of Tiglath-pileser III., *c.* 745 B.C.; Sargon II., *c.* 722 B.C.; and Sennacherib, *c.* 705 B.C.), where the spoils are being brought up and counted, the tablet scribe is always accompanied by a second one, probably an Aramæan, carrying a little wooden palette-block with pens and ink.[1] The palette was provided with two circular recesses, and in one of these the scribe made his black ink by mixing carbon or soot with an aqueous solution of vegetable gum, and in the other his red ink by using a red iron oxide. Hence the scribe is often depicted with two pens behind his ear, one for the black ink and the other for the red. The pens were of the brush type, probably formed by separating and softening the fibres at the end of a reed and trimming them to a point. The whole method, as we have said, was Egyptian, and evidence of this is found in the Book of Ezekiel, where the prophet (9^2. 3. 11^) mentions a man carrying a writer's inkhorn at his girdle. The word which the prophet uses (קֶסֶת) for the outfit, is an adaptation of the Egyptian word *gsty* used for the same. Another proof of the Egyptian origin of such writing is found in the fact that the Egyptian hieratic numerals are employed on the Samaria *ostraka*. In a relief of an Aramæan king of Samal (Zenjirli), dating about a century after the Samaria *ostraka*, a secretary is represented as standing before the king and holding a pen-and-ink outfit, unmis-

[1] Breasted, *American Journal of Semitic Languages and Literatures*, xxxii. (1915–16), p. 245.

takably Egyptian, in his left hand. It is clear that the method went along with the alphabet, and must have been introduced from Egypt about the same time as the latter. In this fact we may see some confirmation of the theory that the latter too was of Egyptian origin.

These *ostraka* from Samaria are the earliest specimens of Hebrew writing (if we except the Gezer agricultural tablet) which have as yet been discovered, and are therefore of great value and interest to the epigraphist and Hebraist. They not only give us geographic and economic details, but reveal the nature of the alphabet in the time of Ahab, several years earlier than the Baal-Lebanon and Moabite inscriptions. The *ostraka* were not intended to be permanent records, but were mere temporary notes, consisting of small accounts of wine and oil for the palace. For particularly important writings papyrus was the material employed, and judging from the five hundred rolls of this which Unamūn took from Egypt to Byblus two centuries before Ahab,[1] there must have been a considerable amount of it in use. Unfortunately, however, papyrus, which has been well preserved in Egypt owing to the dryness of the soil, has not withstood the humidity of the Syrian climate, and thus many original documents and state annals have disappeared for ever. Stone in the form of a stele was occasionally used, but the Israelites, instead of engraving characters

[1] Breasted, *Ancient Records of Egypt*, iv. par. 582.

1

בשת העשרת לשמ
ריו מבארים נבלין
ישן
רגע אלישע 2
עזא ק—בש 1
אלבא----- 1
בעלא אלישע 1
ידעיו 1

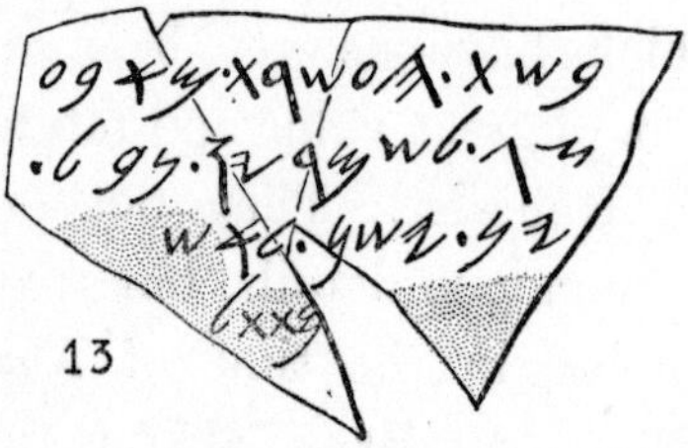

13

בשת העשרת מאבע
זר לשמריו נבל
ין ישן לאשא
-----מתתל

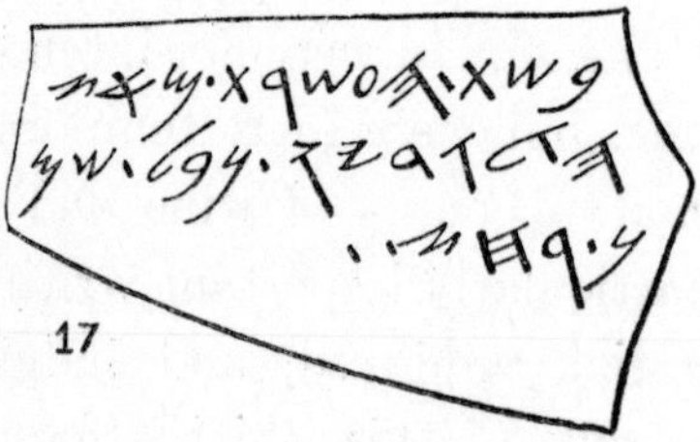

17

בשת העשרת מאז
ה לגדיו נבל שמ
ן רחץ

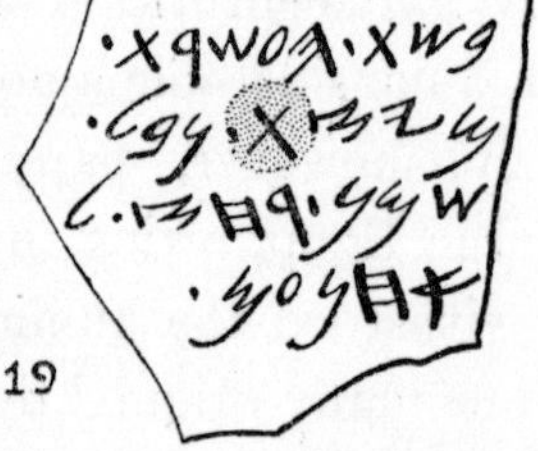

19

בשת העשרת
מיצת נבל
שמן רחץ ל
אחנעם

Ostraka in Facsimile

(From *Excavations*, i. pp. 233 ff.)

Note.—Smaller type in the transcription represents letters lost in the original.

A dot above a letter signifies that the character is doubtful.

Broken lines denote lost letters, where no indication of their character is possible.

on it, preferred to cover it with whitewash (שִׂיד; cf. Dt 27$^{2.4}$), so as to receive impressions in ink. Even this would hardly survive a few inclement seasons, and was a most unsatisfactory method of recording history.[1] For ordinary purposes, especially where economy was an element, potsherds or *ostraka* (חֶרֶשׂ) seem to have been the material, and not only Samaria but Elephantinē has furnished us with numerous specimens. They were usually broken to a suitable shape with a certain amount of skill, and the inscriptions were not written horizontally, as jar labels in pre-Hellenistic times were (always on the upper part of the jar), but at various angles, and the scribe was sometimes forced to split a word at the end of a line or crowd the words together at the end of the inscription, so as to fit the potsherd. Some of the Samaria fragments, each bearing a separate and complete inscription, fit together, and therefore belonged originally to the same jar, which had probably been a broken one and used for potsherd purposes. The excavators have had little difficulty in dating the inscriptions. The words are separated by strokes or points, a distinction recognized as very ancient. The whole circumstances show that they date from the reign of Ahab, and this has been confirmed by the dis-

[1] Surprise has sometimes been expressed at the small number of monumental inscriptions found in Palestine, but the reason lies not only in what we have just said but in the fact that the country was of small political importance compared with Assyro-Babylonia or Egypt and was rarely master of its own destinies.

covery in the same debris of a large two-handled jar of Egyptian alabaster containing two cartouches giving two names and titles of Osorkon II. of Egypt (*c.* 874–856 B.C.), a contemporary of Ahab. The inscriptions are dated the ninth, tenth, and fifteenth year, and one the seventeenth (though no king's name is mentioned in any of them),[1] and if the average of these dates be taken, we may therefore fix them about the thirteenth year, *i.e.* about 862 B.C., being twenty years earlier than the inscription of Moab (*c.* 842). We have already an Israelite jasper seal dating from this period. It is an intaglio found at Megiddo, bearing the epigraph: 'To Shema' servant of Jeroboam,' and having on it a lion of the Assyrian type with open jaws and uplifted tail.[2]

The alphabetical letters used are like those of the oldest known Israelite inscriptions. Letters essentially similar were also found scratched or incised on two Israelite potsherds, one picked up on the surface of a field on the southern slope of the hill, and the other in the debris at the mouth of a cave.[3] Some of the same letters, too, were found on ten large building stones of the Israelite period, and in this case were

[1] Dussaud would translate eleventh and thirteenth instead of fifteenth and seventeenth.

[2] Schumacher, *Tell el-Mutesellim*, i. p. 99. There is a representation of the seal in Driver, *Schweich Lectures*, p. 91. The Jeroboam mentioned was not one of the kings, as Kautzsch thinks (*Mittheilungen und Nachrichten*, 1904, pp. 1–4, 81–83). On this point, cf. *Syria*, 1925, p. 108.

[3] Nos. 64 and 65, *Excavations*, i. p. 243.

probably quarry marks (*vide* p. 15). The following is the alphabet used :

THE OSTRAKA ALPHABET

(From *Excavations*, i. p. 243)

All these ancient characters differ considerably from those of later Hebrew ; and if the earlier documents of the Old Testament were written in them, one can understand the difficulties which the early scribes had to encounter and the mistakes in copying to which they were liable and which they undoubtedly made. Nothing can therefore be more important than the study of early

Semitic epigraphy for the solution of many problems of textual criticism. An examination of the Samaria characters leads to several conclusions :

For one thing, the approximate date of the small agricultural tablet ($4\frac{1}{4}$ by $2\frac{3}{4}$ inches) from Gezer, which Vincent, S. A. Cook, and others would put about the time of the Exile, and which Lidzbarski, Gray, and Ronzevalle have placed in the eighth century B.C., if not in the ninth,[1] must now be fixed earlier still, probably about 900 B.C.[2] The tablet, which is the attempt of some one to group the months according to their agricultural importance, has eight lines in archaic characters throughout. The whole appearance of the script is very ancient. There are no traces of the characteristics of the later Hebrew writing, such as the lengthening and curving of the shafts of the letters, the supplementary additions, and the overlapping, intersection, and prolongation of the strokes. If the characters on it be compared with the Phœnician ones at Byblus in the tenth century[3] and with those on the Samaria *ostraka*, they will be found to be intermediate between these two. For instance, the letters *hêth* (𐤇, 𐤇), *lāmedh* (𐤋, 𐤋), *mêm* (𐤌), and *ṣādhê* (𐤑) are similar to the Phœnician, but not so developed as the Samaria

[1] Cf. *P.E.F. Quarterly Statement*, 1909, pp. 26, 88, 107, 189, 232, 237, 284 ; Vincent, *Revue biblique*, April 1909, pp. 243 ff., 493 ff.

[2] Cf. Dussaud, *Syria*, 1926, pp. 327 f.

[3] For these (the inscription of Abîba'al and that of Elîba'al) see p. 55, n. 1.

The Agricultural Tablet from Gezer

(By permission of the Palestine Exploration Fund)

specimens of these.[1] The same may be said of some of the other letters. On the other hand, *yôdh* (𐤉) and *kaph* (𐤊)[2] are identical with the Samaria characters and thus show progress beyond the Phœnician. As for the *wāw* characters (𐤅𐤅𐤅𐤅), some of them are plainly like the Phœnician specimen (𐤅), while others plainly show an evolution. There are other points of comparison which lead to the same conclusion. Vincent holds that there may be a real difference between alphabetic characters engraved on a stone (like the Abîba'al and Elîba'al ones) and those written on potsherds with a reed pen, and that no conclusions can be drawn from such comparisons. This undoubtedly is so where the characters written with a pen are of the cursive type, but the cursive was a later development and not found as early as the Samaria *ostraka*. In these early ages the form of writing engraved on stones did not differ from the current form traced by pen and ink. The engraver on stone, in applying his tool, only copied the characters as they were traced on potsherds or parchment. This is clearly seen in the inscription on Aḫîrâm's sarcophagus, where the engraver has faithfully followed the fluctuations of the reed. So long as we take care to eliminate admitted deviations from the normal, which after all are very rare and purely accidental, resulting often from want

[1] See Table of Alphabets, facing p. 164.

[2] This letter is doubtful, being taken as a *tāw* by Gray.

of room,[1] we can legitimately compare an engraved inscription with a written one.[2] It is therefore apparent that the Gezer plaque must be assigned to about 900 B.C., rather than later as generally supposed, and this is also evident from its use of *wāw* in place of the definite article (a matter to which we refer below). Seeing that some characters on the plaque exhibit slight changes from the Phœnician, it must have been at this time that the Hebrew writing showed a tendency to deviate from the latter.[3] It was probably at this time also—or a little before it, certainly not later—that the Greeks borrowed their alphabet from Phœnicia.[4]

Thanks to our epigraphists, we have reached a stage of greater certainty now in the evolution of the northern Semitic alphabet. It is now generally agreed that we cannot start from the Babylonian cuneiform writing or the Sumerian picture writing, although Zimmern, Ball, Delitzsch, Hommel, Peters, Deecke, and others have advocated this origin. Hommel, for instance,[5] chooses eight Semitic char-

[1] For example, compare *sāmekh* in *ostrakon* No. 16.

[2] On this point, cf. *Syria*, 1925, p. 327.

[3] The native Phœnician, as it continued, may be seen in the Baal-Lebanon inscription, traced on the rim of a bronze cup found at Cyprus in 1876, and dating from the reign of Hiram II., *c.* 738 B.C. (cf. Contenau, *La Civilization phénicienne*, p. 316). See Table of Alphabets (facing p. 164), col. ix. It is found later (fifth century B.C.) in the long epitaph engraved on the sarcophagus of Eshmunazar, King of Sidon, discovered in 1855.

[4] Cf. *Syria*, 1924, p. 157, and 1925, p. 103.

[5] *Gesch. Bab. u. Assyr.*, pp. 50 ff.

acters which he regards as similar or almost similar to corresponding Babylonian ones, but a comparison of them does not warrant this view. There is little connection observable between any of them, but rather considerable differences. Deecke has easily found among cuneiform characters twenty-two signs on which to base his theory,[1] but as these are taken from very widely separated places and very diverse epochs, the value of his argument is considerably lessened. Mr. L. M. Waddell, an upholder of the Sumerian parentage, bases his view on the theory that the original begetters of the Aryan peoples in race, civilization, and literature, were the Sumerians, and traces back the alphabet to Sumerian non-alphabetic signs.[2] Apart from other difficulties connected with his view, it is most unlikely that the Semites should have adopted an Aryan alphabet, dropping out all the vowels. It is far more probable that the latter people changed the Semitic gutturals, which they could not pronounce and for which they had no use, into vowels.

Nor can we start from the Cyprian script, as Prätorius would have us do, nor from the Minoan or Phæstos ones. According to the Minoan theory, as advocated by Sir Arthur Evans,[3] the Philistines (who belonged originally to Crete) introduced the alphabet into Palestine when they established them-

[1] *Der Ursprung des altsemit. Alphabets.*
[2] *The Aryan Origin of the Alphabet*, Luzac, 1927.
[3] *Scripta Minoa*, vol. i. pp. 77–94 (Oxford, 1909).

selves there in the twelfth century B.C. In Crete thousands of tablets have been discovered bearing inscriptions, some of a linear type and others pictographic, showing that various forms of writing existed in the Ægean world at an early epoch. The origin of these is unknown, but the simplest explanation, and probably the correct one, is that they were imitations of the Egyptian system or influenced in some way by it. The Phæstos script, with which Professor Stewart Macalister compares the Phœnician, is found on a clay disk of about 6 inches in diameter, discovered at Phæstos in Crete. The characters are hieroglyphic, engraved with a ' punch ' of some kind, and represent heads, birds, fishes, flowers, boats—indeed all that constitutes the hieroglyphic material of writing. The disk may be dated from the second half of the second millennium B.C.[1] It is supposed to be of Lycian or Carian origin, and has two faces with the inscription running in spiral form from the circumference to the centre.

Professor Flinders Petrie has found many supporters of his theory that the Phœnician writing developed out of a widely diffused signary in all corners of the Mediterranean littoral.[2] But it is beginning to be evident that Champollion, Salvolini, Van Drival, Lenormant, De Rougé, and other Egyptologists of a past generation were correct

[1] Cf. Dussaud, *Civiliz. pré-hellén.*, 1914, pp. 425 f.

[2] Petrie, *The Formation of the Alphabet* (London, 1912).

when they traced the alphabet to Egypt. It was Lenormant who first suggested a derivation from the Egyptian hieroglyphics, and his pupil Emmanuel De Rougé from the hieratics (the cursive script) of the Early Empire as known to us in the Papyrus Prisse (XIth and XIIth Dynasties). As early as 1859 the latter scholar read a lecture at 'L'Académie des Inscriptions,' in which he endeavoured to establish this relationship.[1] Within recent years, particularly since the discovery of the *Serâbit el-Khâdim* inscriptions (see below), many scholars have come round to Lenormant's view,[2] and it seems now well established that the alphabet had the Egyptian hieroglyphics both for pattern and prototype—for pattern as to its nature, and for prototype as to its outward form.[3] The consonantal signs were developed automatically in course of time from the Egyptian owing to the language disintegrating and consonants being the only parts left of certain

[1] De Rougé, *Mémoire sur l'origine égyptienne de l'alphab. phénic.*, 1874.

[2] Cf. Alan H. Gardiner, *Journal of Egyptian Archæology*, iii. (1916), pp. 1 ff., with Cowley's supplementary remarks; Sethe, *Nachrichten der Königlichen Gesellschaft der Wissenschaften zu Göttingen*, 1916, pp. 88 ff., 1917, pp. 437 ff.; Schaumberger, *Biblica*, vi. (containing the views of Grimme, 1923, and Völter, 1924); Sethe, in *Zeitschr. d. Deut. Morgenl. Ges.*, 1926, v. 24–54.

[3] In 1927, some tablets found at Glozel, 12 miles from Vichy, in France, which were inscribed with Phœnician and other signs said to date from *c.* 4000 B.C., were regarded by some archæologists as evidence that the Phœnician alphabet had originated in the West, but an international commission of experts reported that the tablets were not ancient and had been buried recently. See the writer's exposure of these Glozel finds in *Scotsman*, 27th, 28th, and 29th Dec. 1927.

roots. In this way the Egyptian writing became more closely approximated to an alphabetic system than the Babylonian did. It was probably the Hyksos, as Sethe has lately shown, who turned this fact to good account by inventing the alphabet, and as this Semitic race formed a link between Egypt and Palestine, it is easily seen how the alphabet reached Phœnicia. According to Greek tradition, the inventor was Cadmus, the founder of Grecian civilization, who was believed to be of Phœnician origin; but there may be some truth in the statement of Hecatæus, a Grecian historian who lived during the reign of Ptolemy I. (323–283 B.C.), that Cadmus was one of the leaders of the Hebrews (Hyksos ?) who left Egypt at the time of the Exodus.[1]

This view of the origin of the Phœnician and kindred alphabets is corroborated by decisive facts. As Dr. Alan H. Gardiner has pointed out,[2] the geographical position of Egypt between Syria and Arabia is more favourable than that of any other country. Besides, as the Phœnician alphabet has been found complete and well developed at Byblus as far back as 1250 B.C., many centuries must be allowed for this development from a more primitive type. But the farther back we go, there is the less probability of the source being found in Syria, or Crete, or any country except Egypt or Babylonia;

[1] Hecatæus, in Diodorus, xl. 3 (*Exc. Photii*, pp. 542 ff., French ed.); C. Müller, *Frag. Hist. Græc.*, ii. pp. 384 ff.; Schmidt, in *Recueil d'études égyptologiques*, p. 166.

[2] Gardiner, *Journal of Egyptian Archæology*, iii. (1916), pp. 11 f.

and as the Babylonian cuneiform, which is syllabic and non-alphabetic, cannot have given rise to the Semitic, Egypt seems to be the only likely source. Further, in the Egyptian hieroglyphic script vowels are omitted and a full alphabet of consonants is found, as in Phœnician, Hebrew, and other Semitic languages.[1]

Assuming the correctness of this theory, we have now specimens of several steps or landmarks in the development of the northern Semitic alphabet. First, we have the *Serâbit el-Khâdim* inscriptions, now 15 in number, in primitive Semitic characters, first discovered by Flinders Petrie in the Sinaitic Peninsula, and dated probably from about 1900 B.C. This may be regarded as the proto-Semitic script. Some of the inscriptions appear on small votive offerings of peculiar style, exhumed from the ruins of a temple; while the more important ones, eight in number, are carved in the rock on the plateau a mile and a half west of the temple. The alphabet is the same as that described by Palmer and Weill on a rock in the *Wady Maghâra*, another mining district of Sinai. At first sight the inscriptions appear to consist of roughly graven Egyptian hieroglyphics, but on closer inspection they are seen not to belong to this form of Egyptian writing, though many of the signs are obviously borrowed from it.

[1] Cf. Gardiner, 'The Nature and Development of the Egyptian Hieroglyphic Writing,' in *Journal of Egyptian Archæology*, ii. (1915), pp. 61 ff.; H. Schäfer, 'Die Vokallosigkeit des phönizischen Alphabets,' in *Zeitschrift für ägyptische Sprache*, vol. lii. (1915), pp. 95 ff.

We find the human head, the ox's head, the human eye, the fish, the snake, and other signs drawn evidently from the hieroglyphics and representing alphabetical letters. These inscriptions must not be confused with the graffiti which are to be found in large numbers in the *Wady Mokatteb* and elsewhere, and which belong to the first three centuries of the Christian era. Those we refer to are many centuries older, and undoubtedly contain the earliest Semitic alphabet, much earlier than the Phœnician. The letters seem to be selected arbitrarily, and their value is based on the acrophonic principle, *i.e.* the names of objects represented supplied the letters (thus *bêth* being the word for 'house,' the miniature picture of a house supplied the letter *b*). If the Hyksos invented this alphabet, as seems probable, there is no difficulty in assuming that they brought it to Palestine with them at the beginning of the sixteenth century B.C., where it developed into the Phœnician. It is not unlikely that it is also the parent of the Sabæan, Thamûdenic, Safâitic, and others in the south.[1]

Second in time, we find the Phœnician, which was

[1] For a discussion of the inscriptions, see (in addition to works mentioned on p. 49, n. 2) article by the writer in *Expository Times*, 1926, p. 327 ('Moses and the New Sinai Inscriptions'), with references there and in *Journal of Egyptian Archæology*, Oct. 1926, p. 295; also, in particular, articles by Profs. Lake and Blake, and Prof. Romain F. Butin, S.M., on "The Serâbit Inscriptions," in *Harvard Theol. Review*, Jan. 1928, with bibliography to date there. Lake and Blake visited Serâbit in 1927 and discovered other inscriptions there in the same primitive script.

in current use several centuries later at Byblus, as is evident from the inscription in Aḫîrâm's tomb, dating about 1250 B.C.[1] This inscription is one of the most important of its kind since the Moabite Stone. It was discovered by M. Montet in 1923, and consists of two lines. The date of it is known from the vases and other objects in the tomb (including, for example, a very beautiful Mycenæan ivory), which point to the time of Ramesses II. (*c.* 1301–1234 B.C.).[2] The inscription thus takes us back to the thirteenth century, or if we do not accept the cartouche of Ramesses II. as a *terminus ad quem*, it must date from at least the twelfth. It is therefore beyond dispute that the alphabet was in widespread use in Phœnicia, and not as a mere novelty, at that early date. This is confirmed by the fact that half-way down the shaft leading to the tomb, some writing in the same characters has been rapidly traced on the wall. This writing, which is a real graffito scribbled when the shaft was half-filled, is not the work of an official or scribe but of some ordinary contractor or labourer.

The introduction of the alphabet from Egypt to

[1] Cf. Lidzbarski, *Nachrichten*, Göttingen, 1924, pp. 43 ff.; 'Zu den phönizischen Inschriften von Byblos,' in *Orient. Lit. zeitung*, 1927, cols. 453–458; Dussaud, 'Les Inscriptions phén. du tombeau d'Ahiram,' *Syria*, v. (1924), pp. 135–157, vi. pp. 104 ff.; Vincent, *Revue biblique*, Apr. 1925, pp. 161–193; S. A. Cook, *P.E.F. Quarterly Statement*, Oct. 1925, pp. 210 ff.; Gressmann, *Zeit. f. d. Alttest. Wissenschaft*, 1924, pp. 349 ff.; H. Bauer, *Orient. Lit. zeitung*, Mar. 1925, cols. 129–140.

[2] Cf. Contenau, *La Civiliz. phénic.*, p. 321.

Phœnicia was easy and natural. Not only would the Hyksos carry it there on their dispersion from Egypt in the sixteenth century B.C., but it must be remembered that the Egyptian influence was the principal one in Phœnicia, dating from the very origin of Egyptian history (cf. Gn 10), and continuing during all the period of the Hyksos and later. It was specially strong throughout the course of the second millennium B.C., as is evident from the tombs at *Kafer-ed-Djarra* (near Sidon) and the Tell el-Amarna Letters. There appears to have been some distant connection, too, between *Serâbit el-Khâdim* and Byblus, for in the inscriptions found at the former place mention is made of the Semitic goddess Ba'alath who was worshipped at Byblus.[1]

There is a close similarity between several of the Sinaitic letters and those in Aḫîrâm's inscription. One has only to glance at the following table to notice this :

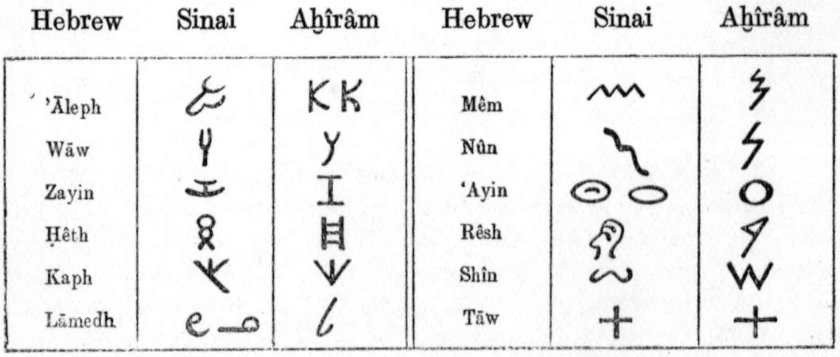
Hebrew
Sinai
Aḫîrâm
Hebrew
Sinai
Aḫîrâm
'Āleph
Wāw
Zayin
Ḥêth
Kaph
Lāmedh
Mêm
Nûn
'Ayin
Rêsh
Shîn
Tāw

[1] Cf. בעלת גבל in the inscription of יחומלך (*Corpus Inscript. Semit.*, t. i. pars. 1, No. 1, ll. 2, 3, 7, and 8, p. 4).

If one should think, as Dussaud, Contenau, and others do, that there is too much difference between the Sinaitic characters and the Phœnician ones in Aḫîrâm's time for them to be related, let it be remembered that a period of about six or seven hundred years intervened during which the signs had abundance of time to develop entirely new characteristics.

Third, about three centuries later, we come to the inscriptions of Abîba'al (*c.* 942 B.C.) and of Elîba'al (*c.* 925 B.C.), both found at Byblus, and exhibiting excellent specimens of the Phœnician alphabet. The Abîba'al inscription is carved upon the base of a granite statuette of Shishak I. (*c.* 947–925 B.C.), and the Elîba'al one occurs on a statue of Osorkon I. (*c.* 925–894 B.C.), successor of Shishak, preserved at the Louvre.[1] To these specimens must be added the inscription on a bronze arrow-head which was recently discovered near *Nabatieh* in the southern Lebanon, and which has been dated by Virolleaud, Dussaud, and others about the tenth century B.C.[2] In all these, there is little difference

[1] For the Abîba'al inscription, cf. Lidzbarski, *Orient. Lit. zeitung*, 1927, cols. 453–458; Clermont-Ganneau, *Recueil d'archéol. orient.*, vi. pp. 74–78 and plate ii.; Dussaud, 'Les. Inscript. phén. du tomb. d'Ahiram,' in *Syria*, v. (1924), pp. 145 ff. and plate xlii.; *Revue biblique*, July 1926, pp. 321 ff. For the Elîba'al one, cf. Lidzbarski, as cited above; Dussaud, *Syria*, vi. (1925), pp. 101 ff.; C. C. Torrey, *Journal of American Oriental Society*, Sept. 1926; *Revue biblique*, July 1926, pp. 323 ff.

[2] Cf. Paul-Emile Guigues, 'Pointe de flèche,' and Ronzevalle, 'Note sur le texte phénicien de la flèche, etc.,' in *Mélanges de l'Université Saint-Joseph*, xi. No. 7 (Beyrouth, 1926); Dussaud, *Syria*, viii. (1927), p. 185.

in the letters from those in Aḫîrâm's time. Only a few show some characteristic changes.

Fourth, we have the Gezer tablet, the first Hebrew writing so far known to us, and dating, as we have suggested, from about 900 B.C.

Fifth, there are the inscriptions on the Samaria *ostraka* (*c.* 862 B.C.), also in Hebrew.

Sixth, coming farther down history, we possess the valuable inscription of Mesha on the Moabite Stone, *c.* 842 B.C. Moab and Israel were in close proximity, and the language of this Stone is almost identical with Hebrew, apart from a few dialectical variations.

Seventh, there is the Siloam inscription, consisting of six lines in Hebrew, engraved in a recess of the Ophel Tunnel, and attributed to the reign of Hezekiah (*c.* 700 B.C.) or Manasseh (*c.* 650 B.C.).

Eighth, we now have an excellent Phœnician inscription on an ivory box-lid, discovered in 1927 below the pavement of E-Nun-Maḫ, the treasury house of the Moon God at Ur in Babylonia, by the University of Pennsylvania excavators. This inscription, which states that the box is a gift to the goddess Astarte, must be dated sometime during the reign of Nebuchadrezzar (*c.* 605–562 B.C.), who constructed the pavement.[1] From the year 800 B.C. onward we have also numer-

[1] For a copy of the inscription, see the Pennsylvania *Museum Journal*, June 1927, p. 134.

ous Israelite seals containing the Phœnician characters.[1]

The difference in the notation between the definite article in the Gezer plaque and in the Samaria *ostraka* is another point worth noting, to which Dussaud and others have drawn attention.[2] In the former, *wāw* is employed, as ירחו אסף ('month of the fruit harvest'), ירחו לקש ('month of the after-grass'), etc., while in the latter we have *he*, as בשת התשעת ('in the ninth year'), הין ('the wine,' for הַיַּיִן), היהדי ('the Judæan'), etc. The *wāw* seems to show that the language at the beginning of the ninth century was at least hesitating as to the notation to be adopted for the article (there was none in Phœnician writing), whereas about a quarter of a century later, judging from the *ostraka*, the choice had become definitely fixed on *he*. We know that originally *wāw* was not a mere copulative conjunction but had binding force and was sometimes applied in this sense to denote juxtaposition or connection.[3] This use of it, as Professor G. Hoffmann has pointed out, made the second noun definite, so that *wāw* easily took the place of the definite article, afterwards passing into *he* and being generalized and applied to independent words. The *wāw*, therefore, in such an expression as ירחו אסף on the

[1] A list of these, with the alphabet, is given in Dussaud, *Samarie au temps d'Achab*, pp. 334 ff.

[2] Cf. Lidzbarski, *Ephem. für Semit. Epigraphik*, iii. pp. 36 ff., 279 ff.

[3] Cf. Driver, *Hebrew Tenses*, p. 122.

Gezer plaque is the so-called *wāw compaginis*, and must be read as יֶרַח הָאָסִף ('month of the fruit harvest'). The sign cannot be meant, as Vincent suggested, for *nûn* (נ), a form of the plural occurring in such dialects as Arabic and Aramaic, and also on the Moabite Stone. It is everywhere a *wāw* and nothing else, as Lidzbarski, Gray, Ronzevalle, and other Semitic epigraphists have demonstrated. Nor can it be taken in its usual conjunctive sense, as this would not suit its position in any of the five places where it occurs. From the context, one could only expect the article ה, and it is noteworthy that the *wāw* sign appears in the southern Semitic writing as a ה. We have some instances of this *wāw compaginis* in the Old Testament, in poetic cases or elevated language, as in Gn 1^{24}, חַיְתוֹ־אֶרֶץ ('beast of the earth'), a form which is replaced in v.^{25} by חַיַּת הָאָרֶץ, showing that both forms are syntactically alike (cf. also Ps 50^{10} 79^{2} $104^{11.\,20}$, Is $56^{9.\,9}$, Zp 2^{14}). G. R. Driver takes the *wāw* in such cases to be an old termination for the nominative singular,[1] but while this may have been one of the original uses of the letter, its replacement in v.^{25} by *hē* (inadvertently omitted by him in his quotation from this verse) shows that it had the determinative force to which we refer. In the Gezer inscription the *wāw* is absent in those cases where the following noun could not have had the definite article, except in one case

[1] *The People and the Book*, p. 83.

(l. 7) where its absence is evidently due to the inexperience of the writer, who appears to have been a simple peasant. The Assyrian and the Ethiopic did not develop in the same way as Hebrew and consequently have no definite article, while Aramaic and Sabæan took quite a different direction from Hebrew, the former adding *-â* to the end of a word and the latter *-n* for this purpose. Of the Semitic languages, only Arabic agrees with Hebrew in the possession of a definite article prefixed to the word, although, if the view just expressed be correct, its origin could not have been the same as that of the Hebrew article.

These changes in Hebrew writing by the time of Ahab, including the deviations from the Phœnician, show not only considerable intellectual and literary development but a lengthy process of evolution. It is probable that the Israelites had been in possession of writing for many ages before this, and had made constant use of it. We cannot be guided in this matter by the lack of literary and other documents, for it is known that papyrus, which was the material on which important texts were written, has not withstood the climate of Palestine. The *argumentum e silentio* is therefore valueless in such a case. Moses, having been brought up in the Egyptian court, was probably acquainted with the art of writing, although of course this proves nothing as to his actual authorship of any Old Testament documents. The name Kiriath-Sepher (also called

Kiriath-Sannah and Debir) ostensibly means 'city of writing' or 'city of books,' and it has been conjectured that this Judæan town, which is known from the Payprus Anastasi I. to have been in existence in the thirteenth century B.C., contained a library (perhaps something like that of Ashurbanipal at Nineveh) or record office. In the Book of Judges, whose composition may be said to date from about the ninth century B.C., we read that some youth wrote down for Gideon the names of seventy-seven citizens of the town of Succoth (8^{14}). Samuel is said to have written a description of the first Israelite kingdom in a book (סֵפֶר). Solomon, we are told, had two scribes or secretaries of State who looked after the political correspondence (1 K 4^{3}). David wrote a letter to Joab, and there were certainly State annalists in his reign (2 S 8^{16} 20^{25}), and probably records going back to a remote period. All such documents were probably written in the primitive Semitic alphabet to which we have referred. According to Hugh Winckler, Dr. Naville, Benzinger, and others, the cuneiform was the official mode of writing in the two kingdoms up to the time of Hezekiah (*c.* 719–692 B.C.).[1] It is said that some parts of the Old Testament were written in cuneiform and on clay tablets, and certain Biblical terms have been

[1] Winckler, *Altoriental. Forschungen*, iii. 1902, pp. 165 ff.; Naville, *Archæology of the Old Testament* (also *Schweich Lectures*); Benzinger, *Hebr. Archæol.*, 2nd ed. p. 176; Jeremias, *Das alte Testament in Lichte des alten Orients*, p. 263; H. Grimme, *Orient. Lit. zeitung*, x. cols. 610–615.

interpreted accordingly. Naville, in fact, argues that 'Moses wrote in Babylonian cuneiform those books which are attributed to him, and of which he is the probable author.' [1] Dr. A. E. Cowley too, in his discussion of the Elephantinē papyri,[2] holds that the documents which eventually formed part of the Torah were written in cuneiform and probably in the Babylonian language. It was Ezra, he believes, who, with the assistance of his colleagues, translated the cuneiform documents into Hebrew, and wrote the result down in the simple Aramaic alphabet. But there is no evidence for such views. The cuneiform, which was better adapted than the Egyptian for writing Semitic, was undoubtedly employed in Canaan in the fourteenth century B.C. as the diplomatic mode of writing (according to the Tell el-Amarna Letters) [3] and for official intercommunication in Palestine (according to writings found at Lachish and Taanach), but this does not prove anything positively, for such a mode of writing

[1] Naville, *The Discovery of the Book of the Law*, p. 40.

[2] Cowley, *The Aramaic Papyri of the Fifth Century B.C.* (1923).

[3] The language of these letters, though written in cuneiform, is not pure Babylonian, as some scholars assume, but appears to be a form of Amorite fused with Canaanite. The vowel *a*, for instance, which is characteristic of the Amorite dialect, is used for the Babylonian *i* in the prefix of the imperfect and in other cases. The letter *t* occurs instead of *k* as the pronominal affix in the 1st pers. sing. perf., as *naṣrâti*, 'I have preserved,' for *naṣrâki*. The prefix *ya-* or *yi-* is used in place of *i* in the 3rd pers. sing. masc. of the imperf., as *yamlik* or *yimluk*, 'he takes counsel,' for *imlik*. There are important differences in the syntax too. It is the pure Babylonian words that are explained by Canaanite glosses, of which there are nearly one hundred (cf. Driver, *The People and the Book*, pp. 105 f.).

may have been used only because the clay tablets required for it were practically indestructible. The communications they contained were generally of such a nature that their preservation was desirable. Besides, the want of fine clay in Palestine must have been an insuperable difficulty in the employment of such a script for ordinary correspondence. The importation of clay for the use of diplomats or official scribes must have been expensive, and any kind of writing material within reach would have to serve the ordinary writer. The cuneiform could not have been within every one's reach, and must only have been retained with difficulty. In the Tell el-Amarna Letters the writer had often to address his words, not to his correspondent personally, but to the latter's scribe, because this man alone could read what was written. We have a parallel case (though connected with language, not with script) in English history, for Acts of Parliament and certain legal documents were inscribed in Norman-French for several centuries after this language had ceased to hold the chief place, and at the very time that Chaucer, Wyclif, and others were writing in English. Similarly, in Ireland, until about five centuries ago, Government documents were written in Norman-French or English, yet all the while there was the splendid Celtic literature dating from before the English Conquest. How long the cuneiform continued in Palestine is unknown. It could only have had the chief place during the Babylonian supremacy. Two contract tablets in cuneiform, dated *c.* 650 B.C., and containing Hebrew names, have been unearthed at Gezer, but as Palestine at that time formed part of the Assyrian empire, they may have come from a local Assyrian garrison or colony. At all events, it was not strange that legal contracts should be written in the script which represented the suzerain power; but this does not prove that the ordinary literary activities of the land were not carried on in the Semitic alphabet. For everyday purposes the former method of writing could have had no domination over the latter, especially after the Israelites secured possession of the land. During the Israelite monarchy at least, the latter must have been the official mode of writing. The Israelites must have used it constantly for this purpose generations before Ahab reigned in Israel or Mesha in Moab. Naville's statement that the Phœnician alphabet was not introduced into Palestine till the age of David [1] is now known to be far from correct, and the same must be said of the recent statement of Meinhold that the most ancient written literature of the Hebrews began in the time of Solomon,[2] for evidence shows that the alphabet must have been well known in Palestine some centuries before the time of these kings. According to the discoveries at Byblus, the Phœnician alphabet, with which the ancient Hebrew one has such a close

[1] Naville, *The Discovery of the Book of the Law*, p. viii.

[2] Meinhold, *Einführung in das alte Testament*, Giessen, 1926.

connection, was in a perfect condition by the thirteenth century B.C., and must have been widely used even at that early epoch. The exigencies of trade demanded its use. With its twenty-two simple characters, it must have been much easier to write than the intricate cuneiform syllabary with its hundreds of signs, syllabic, polyphonic, and ideographic.[1]

[1] For further reasons upholding this view, cf. Chapman, *Introduction to the Pentateuch* (1911), pp. 320–322; G. A. Cooke, 'Was Deuteronomy written in Cuneiform?' in the *Interpreter*, July 1912, pp. 380 ff.; W. Erbt, *Orient. Lit. zeitung*, xi. cols. 57–62; Paul Haupt, *ibid.* cols. 119–125; E. König, *ibid.* cols. 125–127; Cheyne, *ibid.* col. 195.

CHAPTER IV

THE LOCALITIES MENTIONED

On the north the kingdom of Israel in its palmiest days touched the slopes of Hermon and the Lebanon. But the boundary was uncertain.[1] Some scholars would fix it a little south of Lebanon.[2] Others again would include Lebanon or part of it.[3] There seems to have been no real line of demarcation, and the boundary probably oscillated from reign to reign and even from year to year. Carmel, at all events, which is separated from the Central Range by a softer formation, was not an integral part of the kingdom, being held sometimes by Phœnicia and sometimes by Israel. On the south, the Vale of Aijalon and the gorge of Michmash (*Wady Suweinîṭ*) formed the natural line. This was a real pass across the mountain range, bringing the Maritime Plain and the Jordan Valley into close connection, and was in all ages a regular caravan route (the Crusaders used it). But the boundary appears to have varied here also. It certainly went as far as Bethel, which

[1] Cf. Gray, *Numbers*, pp. 458–462.

[2] Cf. Van Kasteren, *Revue biblique*, 1895, pp. 23 ff.

[3] Cf. Furrer, in *Zeit. des Deutsch. Pal. Ver.*, viii. 27–29.

it included (for Bethel was a sanctuary of North Israel), and sometimes as far as Geba, 5 miles more to the south (1 K 15^{22}, 2 K 23^{8}). It also included Jericho (1 K 16^{34}, 2 K 2^{4}), and indeed went as far in this south-eastern direction as the north end of the Dead Sea. In the south-western direction it never went beyond the Vale of Aijalon, for there the Philistines were always very strong and indeed held Gibbethon to the north of Aijalon (1 K $16^{15ff.}$). On the east the kingdom included the transjordanic lands of Reuben, Gad, and the half of Manasseh.[1] Omri, indeed, held East Palestine as far north as Bashan and as far south as Mêdeba, Yaḥaṣ, and ʻAṭaroth, and probably the Arnon. These provinces on the east, however, were held on a very precarious tenure, for Ramoth-Gilead (? *er-Remṭeh*, 7 miles south-west of Edrei) and probably Bashan were taken possession of later by the Aramæan kingdom of Damascus, and some of the territories of Reuben and Gad were claimed by Mesha of Moab according to the statement on his monument. Indeed, the eastern frontier of Israel advanced or receded as the powers of these other kingdoms waxed or waned. Later on, owing to the Assyrian menace, Israel must have been confined pretty much to the west of the Jordan, for the Assyrian monarch Tiglath-pileser III. (*c.* 745 B.C.) absorbed Bashan, Gilead, and the rest of

[1] None of the older documents, such as the JE ones, mentions the extension of Manasseh east of the Jordan, but it is stated by the Deuteronomist.

the eastern lands in his empire. If we exclude the uncertain territory north of Esdraelon, the doubtful provinces east of the Jordan, and the lands of Carmel on the west, the whole kingdom was only some 40 miles north and south by some 35 miles east and west—not any larger, indeed, than an average English county.[1] Yet it is packed full of history and romance. It was here that the patriarchs first came (to Shechem), here on Mount Ephraim were the earliest sites of Israelite worship, here the first prophets and heroes arose, and here originated some of the finest of the Hebrew national lyrics. The Old Testament record would be poor without the fields of Dothan, the palm tree of Deborah, the wine-press of Ophrah, the scenes at Carmel and Gilboa, the vineyard of Naboth, the sudden appearances of Elijah, the constant struggles between Baal and Yahweh, the furious driving of Jehu, and the battles with the Assyrians.

One can hardly look at this northern territory on the map without noticing its difference from that of Judah. 'The northern is as fair and open,' says Sir George A. Smith, 'as the southern is secluded and austere, and their fortunes correspond.'[2] The openness of the northern, in fact, is its most noticeable feature. It is rich in vales, meadows, and spacious plains, as contrasted with the steep, tortuous tracks of Judah. Hence the chariot had more scope

[1] Smith, *Historical Geography of the Holy Land*, p. 325.
[2] *Op. cit.* p. 323.

and is mentioned frequently in its history, whereas in the annals of Judah we find only two meagre references to chariot-driving (2 K 9^{28}, 2 Ch 35^{24}). Hence also the northern kingdom stood nearer to the world, as it were, and thus came more in contact with other nations (Phœnicians, Aramæans, Hittites, Assyrians, etc.), and was more influenced by surrounding heathenism.[1] The sins charged against it by the prophets are those that come from a loose civilization—cruelty, drunkenness, luxury, greed, and imitation of foreign cults. It was more connected, too, with the eastern regions across the Jordan, for the passage from it to Gilead was comparatively easy at several places (where valleys led down to fords), whereas Judah was separated from the east by the great barrier of the Dead Sea.

The Samaria *ostraka* mention twenty-one or twenty-two place-names in the northern kingdom. If it be true, as a German scholar has said, that 'geography is latent history,'[2] a good deal may be gleaned from a study of these localities. One particularly interesting fact for the Biblical critic, pointed out by Reisner, is that six of these names are found in Numbers (26^{30-33}) and Joshua ($17^{2, 3}$) as names of clans or tribal divisions in Manasseh. It may be that some of these names of towns and

[1] It was not only the Baalim of Phœnicia that found an easy access. Even the Philistines were able to have a temple of Dagon (*Beit Dejan*) 6½ miles south-east of Shechem.

[2] Rudolph von Ihering, *Vorgeschichte der Indoeuropäer* (1894), p. 97.

villages arose from the Manasseh clans having first colonized them, for many place-names in Palestine have arisen in a similar way. Seeing, however, that they were clearly in existence as *localities* as far back as Ahab's time (*c.* 875), the probability is that the redactor, who certainly lived after this time, took them to represent or account for the clans. The six names referred to are Abi'ezer (אבעזר), Ḥeleḳ (חלק), Shechem (שכם), Shemîda' (שמידע), No'ah (נעה), and Ḥoglah (חגלה). As the first four have a masculine termination, and the remaining two a feminine one, he has included the former among the male descendants and the latter among the female. Thus, according to Joshua's genealogy the first four (along with other three, Asriel, Ḥepher, and Machir, doubtless towns also) are 'sons' of Manasseh; in P these four (along with Asriel and Ḥepher) are sons of Gilead, who is given as a grandson of Manasseh, while the two last (along with Maḥlah, Milcah, and Tirṣah, towns also) are 'daughters' of Zelophehad, a grandson of Gilead. It is apparent that such genealogical schemes are different attempts to correlate and account for the names of the localities referred to. Long ago Kuenen pronounced Zelophehad's 'daughters' to be really towns, but it has been left to these *ostraka* to prove definitely not only this but that Manasseh's 'sons' are towns also. The incorrectness of the redactor is manifest from the mention of Shechem, a name which has easily been identified with the town of

Shechem (Roman Neapolis, modern *Nâblus*).[1] As this town is referred to in the Papyrus Anastasi I. as far back as the XIXth Egyptian Dynasty (*c.* 1321–1210 B.C.),[2] and even in the Tell el-Amarna Letters (*c.* 1400 B.C.),[3] and as excavators have revealed its existence (if it be identical with *Balâṭa*) in earlier ages still, it is clear that one cannot find in it the name of a son of Gilead; and it can hardly be doubted that the remaining names are not those of persons either, but of places, estates, or tribal districts.

The identification of several of the towns mentioned on the *ostraka* has been satisfactorily made by Dussaud,[4] Père Abel,[5] Albright,[6] and others.

[1] Although Shechem is generally located at modern *Nâblus*, the 'Tower of Shechem' is now identified with *Balâṭa*, a small mound about a mile east of it, at the extremity of the valley. In 1926 several scientific societies, American, German, and Dutch, with the assistance of Professor Fr. Böhl, Professor Praschniker, and others, succeeded in laying it bare, including the large rampart, a palace, a sanctuary of the middle Bronze Age, a temple of the period of the Judges, two cuneiform tablets, several objects of worship, some jewellery, and a large and varied quantity of pottery (cf. *Zeitschr. d. deut. Palästina-Vereins*, xlix. (1926), pp. 229 ff.). In 1928 Dr. Welter, excavating on behalf of the German Archæological Institute, discovered what is believed to be the Tower (Jg 9[46ff.]), a remarkably blunt-topped pyramid crowned by a chamber 85 feet by 68 feet, with walls 16 feet thick (cf. *P.E.F. Quarterly*, Jan. 1929, April 1929). The whole enclosure seems to have had a circumference, almost circular, of about 820 yards. The site strikingly confirms the accuracy of the O.T. narrative, according to which the 'Tower of Shechem' lay *outside* and east of the city.

[2] Cf. Gardiner, *Egyptian Hieratic Texts*, i. 1, *The Papyrus Anastasi I.*

[3] Knudtzon, No. 289.

[4] 'Samarie au temps d'Achab,' in *Syria* (1926), i. pp. 9 ff.

[5] *Revue biblique* (1911), pp. 290 ff.

[6] *Journal of Palestine Oriental Society*, v. (1925), pp. 38 ff.

Only a few are unknown or doubtful. Of the five others referred to above:

Abiʿezer (which appears as 'Jeezer' in Nu 26^{30} owing to the *bêth* having disappeared) seems to be identical with the Abisaros of Josephus,[1] modern *el-Bizariah*, 3 miles north-west of Samaria. Guérin found it to be a village of about a hundred inhabitants, on a hill, surrounded with gardens containing pomegranates and fig trees.[2] If this identification be correct, the town may have been known as ʿOphrah at first, for the Abiezrite clan is said to have been settled in the latter place (Jg $6^{11.\ 24}$), which disappears from the Biblical records after Samuel's time.[3]

Noʿah, which is probably the same as Neʿah (Jos 19^{13}), is believed to be the New Testament Nain (*Naΐν*, Lk 7^{11}), the modern *Nein*, placed by Eusebius and St. Jerome in the neighbourhood of ʿEndôr,[4] which belonged to Manasseh (Jos 17^{11}). Owing to the influence of the Greek pronunciation, the *ʿayin* has disappeared (though it remains in the Talmud, Naʿim),[5] as it has also in ʿEndor (modern *Endôr*).

Ḥoglah ('partridge') may be *Ḳuryet Ḥajjâ*, 8 miles west of *Nâblus* (assuming the assimilation of

[1] *Antiq.* VI. xiii. 8.
[2] Guérin, *Samarie*, ii. p. 214.
[3] Ophrah has generally been placed at *eṭ-Ṭaiyibeh*, 4 miles north-east of Bethel, though a few scholars would locate it at *Tell Fârʿah*, about 8 miles east of Samaria.
[4] *Onomasticon*, 94. 23, and 40. 3.
[5] Neubauer, *Géogr. du Talmud*, p. 188.

gîmel and *lāmedh*). This accords with the fact that the same deputy who had charge of Shechem (if we suppose that Shechem is to be supplied on *ostrakon* No. 43, as Reisner thinks)[1] also received consignments from Ḥoglah. On this account there is considerable difficulty in identifying the place with Beth-Ḥoglah (Jos 15^{6} 18^{19}), modern *Ḳaṣr Ḥajlah*, south-east of Jericho, although this site, if not actually within Manasseh's territory (the boundary of which was nowhere precise), must have been only 4 or 5 miles beyond it, and may easily have belonged to this tribe.

Ḥeleḳ has not been identified, but it must have been in the neighbourhood of Ḥaṣerot (*'Aṣîret el-Ḥaṭâb*), south-east of Samaria, for no less than three or four of the senders of contributions to Ahab's palace from Ḥeleḳ (*ostraka* Nos. 22–26) are stated to belong to Ḥaṣerot. Ḥeleḳ is one of the towns mentioned in some Egyptian texts dating from the close of the XIth Dynasty (*c.* 2000 B.C.) reviewed and annotated by Kurt Sethe and R. Dussaud.[2] It is apparent that it had been in existence over a thousand years before Ahab, and is thus another proof that the redactor had taken the names of towns to represent Manasseh's 'sons.' The names, indeed, of its two chiefs are given in the texts referred to.

[1] Nos. 43 and 44 fit together, and Shechem occurs on the latter.

[2] Sethe, *Abhandl. Berl. Akad.*, 1926, philos.-hist. Klasse, Nr. 5, Berlin; Dussaud, *Syria*, VIII. iii. p. 216 f.

Shemîdaʿ has not been identified so far, though attempts have been made by scholars.

Of the sons of Manasseh not mentioned on the *ostraka*, Asriel is no doubt *Oṣarin*, 7 miles south of Shechem (cf. Jezreel = *Zerʿîn*, and *Beit Jibril* = *Beit Jibrîn*, the Arabic *l* and *n* often interchanging).

Ḥepher is doubtless the Canaanite town referred to in Joshua as possessing a king before the arrival of the Israelites (12^{17}). It is probably the same also as the district assigned to the charge of one of Solomon's stewards, Ben-Ḥesed (1 K 4^{10}), which no doubt corresponded to the limits of this ancient kingdom. As this steward lived in Arruboth, which has been identified with *ʿArrâbeh*, about 9 miles north of Samaria (the initial א in Arruboth easily becomes ע owing to the influence of the common place-name ʿArabah),[1] the Ḥepher mentioned is probably *Ḥafireh*, about 2 miles east of Arruboth. This place seems more likely than *Ḥafura*, to the south-west of *Nâblus*.[2] Ḥepher must not be confused with Ḥapharaim, a town of Issachar (Jos 19^{19}), the Egyptian Ḥapuruma,[3] which has been placed by some scholars at *el-ʿAfûleh*, 3 miles west of Shunem

[1] Some scholars would place Arruboth at Rabbith (*Râbâ*), 13 miles north-east of Samaria, but this is too far away to suit the administrative district referred to, which included Socoh, a place identified almost certainly with *Shuweikeh*, about 11 miles north-west of Samaria. Rabbith rather goes back to some form of name like 'Rabbah,' especially as the ruined fortress immediately to the east is called *Khurbet Rabrâbah* (Aram. *rabrâbâ*, 'very great').

[2] For *Ḥafireh* and *Ḥafura*, see Chauvet and Isambert, *Syrie*, p. 407.

[3] Cf. Max Müller, *Asien und Europa*, pp. 158, 170.

(modern *Sôlam*),[1] but corresponds more exactly with *Khurbet Farrîyeh*, the 'Aphraia of Eusebius, an ancient town with remarkable tombs on the low hills south of Carmel.[2]

Of the daughters not mentioned, Maḥlah may be *Makhna el-Fûka*, the name of some ruins on a hill 3 miles south of Shechem, or *Makhna et-Thata*, the name of some ruins in the adjoining plain.[3] Milkah (cf. 1 Ch 7[18], where the ancient feminine Moleketh or Milkat occurs) is doubtless *Merkeh*, a mile or two south of Ḥepher. Tirṣah, which was the residence of the kings of Israel from Jeroboam to Omri, is identified by Robinson, Guérin, Dussaud, A. Socin, and others with *Ṭallûzah*, east of Samaria, on the main road (*via* Thebez, modern *Tûbâṣ*) from Shechem to Beth-shean. It is located by Buhl[4] at *eṭ-Ṭireh*, the Tirathana of Josephus, in the neighbourhood of Mount Gerizim,[5] but it certainly corresponds better with *Ṭallûzah*, a town whose site and strategic position must have made it important in ancient times. Corroboration of this is found in the account of the monk Burchard, who visited Palestine in 1283 and who found the ancient name Tirṣah applied at that time to a town a little east of Samaria. He says: 'De Samaria quattuor leucis contra orientem sita est Thersa civitas, in monte alto; in qua reges Israel, ante constructionem Samarie,

[1] Cf. Baedeker-Socin, *Pal.*[2], p. 238.
[2] Cf. *Onomasticon*, s. Aphraim; Buhl, *Geogr. des alten Pal.*, p. 210.
[3] Guérin, *Samarie*, i. pp. 459 ff.
[4] *Op. cit.* p. 203.
[5] *Antiq.* XVIII. iv. 1.

aliquanto tempore regnaverunt. Et erat in sorte Manasse.' [1] The position and site indicated by Burchard correspond exactly to that of *Ṭallûzah*, except that the distance of four leagues which he gives from Samaria is rather large, the real distance being not more than three. It must be remembered, however, that a 'league' in the Middle Ages was rather indefinite and variable. It would be strange if this important town were not mentioned in the history of Israel.

Of the numerous place-names on the *ostraka* beyond those we have referred to, the identification of several are certain or at least probable. The writer gives them here in alphabetical order :

'Asharot is a doubtful place-name. The incomplete state of the inscription (No. 42) makes it possible to read מעשרת, 'tithes.'

Azzah (or Azah) is identified by Abel with *Zawâtâ*, between *Nâblus* and Samaria, and in this he is supported by Albright and other scholars. Dussaud prefers *'Anzah* (or *'Anazah*), 6 miles north of Samaria, a place probably identical with Inzata of the Egyptian lists.[2] It is a small village on a hill and enclosed with olive trees.[3] But this place is unsuitable, for Azzah was in the same prefecture as Ḳeṣeh and Ḥaṣerot, which lay south of Samaria.

[1] Burchardus de Monte Sion, *Descriptio Terræ Sanctæ*, p. 54 (ed. Laurent).

[2] H. Gautier, *Dict. Géogr.*, i. p. 170 ; *Syria* (1925), p. 344, note 1.

[3] Cf. Guérin, *Samarie*, p. 217.

Be'er-yam is of uncertain vocalization in the second term, but assuming it to be correct this name might mean 'well of the sea,' or 'west well.' Dussaud identifies it with Beer, to which Jonathan ran away to escape from the Shechemites (Jg 9^{21}), and takes this to be *el-Bireh* near *Kaukab el-Hawâ*, and about 8 miles south-west of the Sea of Tiberias.[1] The difficulty about *el-Bireh* is that it is about 30 miles distant from Samaria, though according to Robinson[2] it was even in modern times in the administrative district of *Jenîn* (Engannim). In the writer's view the probability is that Be'er-yam must be sought for somewhere in the vicinity of Abi'ezer, Etpar'an, and Ha-Tell, *i.e.* a few miles north-west of Samaria, for it is included in the same steward's prefecture as these places.

Elmattan (or Elmattôn), the vocalization of which is a little uncertain, seems to be the same as *Elmetin*, which is found on the French military map, about 15 miles south-west of *Nâblus*, although some suggest *Amâtin* (*Ammâtin*), 6 miles south-west of *Nâblus*.

Etpar'an, which occurs on *ostrakon* No. 14 (broken in three pieces), is translated Azat-Par'an or Obot-Par'an by Reisner. Several of the letters are certainly doubtful, but there seems no necessity to insert ז or ב. The place probably corresponds

[1] Some suppose Beer to be the same as Beeroth (Jos 9^{17}), but the latter place was in Benjamin's territory, and as Jonathan's people belonged to Manasseh, he probably fled northward.

[2] *Palæstina*, iii. p. 880.

with *Fer'ôn*, 10 miles west of Samaria, situated on a high and oblong hill and having in Guérin's time a population of about five hundred.[1] This is much preferable to Albright's identification with *Tell Fâr'ah*, east of Samaria. Etpar'an was probably one of the strongholds guarding the passes which emerged on Sharon.[2]

Gib . . ., which is the only part of the name decipherable, may doubtless be completed to Gibe'a ('hill'), probably modern *Jeba'*, 4 miles north of Samaria, on the road which led from the latter place to Jezreel. This seems better than identifying it with Gibeath-Phinehas, 'hill of Phinehas' (Jos 24^{33}), which Conder and Schwarz take to be *'Awertah*, about 5 miles south of *Nâblus*, and which Guérin, trusting to Jerome, places at *Jîbîa*, about 7 miles north-west of Bethel.[3]

Ḥaṣerot must be identified with *'Aṣîret el-Ḥaṭab* (Esora), 2 miles north of Shechem, for it is included with Ḳeṣeh, Azzah, and Saḳ in the district of one steward (Gaddiyo), which seems to have lain between Shechem and Samaria. This rules out an identification with *'Aṣîret el-Ḳiblîyeh*, 4 miles south-west of Shechem, or with *'Aṭṭara* (formerly 'Aṭṭaroth), about 4 miles north-west of Samaria. The last-named place is probably the village Aṭaroth referred to by Eusebius of Cæsarea and by Jerome in the

[1] *Samarie*, ii. p. 352.

[2] Smith, *Historical Geography of the Holy Land*, p. 350.

[3] Conder, *P.E.F. Mem.*, ii. p. 218; Schwarz, *History of Israel*, p. 118; Guérin, *Judée*, iii. pp. 37 f.; Jerome, *Ep.*, i. p. 888.

Onomasticon as being 4 miles from *Sebustieh.*[1] The identification with *'Aṣîret el-Ḥaṭab* is not precluded by the change of *hêth* into *'ayin*, for this is explainable after the lapse of so many years, and is of frequent occurrence. The two sounds correspond to each other, the former being the voiceless form and the latter the voiced.[2]

Kerm Ha-Tell, 'vineyard or estate of Ha-Tell,' which occurs on five of the *ostraka* (Nos. 20, 53, 54, 58, 61), may be a separate place from Ha-Tell (No. 56). If we allow for the popular transformations which sometimes take place in compound names, the former seems to correspond to *Ṭûl Keram*, a large village on the summit of a hill 10 miles west of Samaria.[3] The latter is probably *Attil*, about 5 miles north-east of *Ṭûl Keram*, for it seems to have been included in the same steward's prefecture as Abi'ezer and Etpar'an, and thus can hardly have been *Till*, about 3 miles south-west of *Nâblus*.[4]

Kerm Yeḥu'ali, 'vineyard of Yeḥu'ali,' cannot so far be identified.

Ḳeṣeh (or Ḳôṣoh, like Sôcoh ?) is placed by Abel at *Ḳûsein*, 3 miles south of Samaria,[5] and by Dussaud at *Ḳûzah* (Chusi), about 6 miles south of Shechem.

[1] Eusebius says: *Ἀταρώθ, φυλῆς Ἐφραΐμ· καὶ νῦν εστὶ κώμη Ἀταρὼθ ἐν ὁρίοις Σεβαστῆς, ὡς ἀπὸ δ' μιλίων.* Jerome, in his translation, adds this further detail: 'Nunc vicus ad aquilonem Sebastæ, in quarto ejus milliaris, Atharus dicitur (cf. Ed. Klostermann, 26. 19; P. Thomsen, *Loca Sancta*, p. 29).

[2] Cf. Beth-ḥoron=*Beit-'ur*, Ḥaṣor=*'Asûr*, Ḥolon=*'Alin*, etc.

[3] Cf. Guérin, *Samarie*, p. 353.

[4] Cf. Guérin, *op. cit.* pp. 35, 178.

[5] *Ibid.* p. 211.

If nearness to Samaria be taken into account, the former identification seems preferable.

Saḳ (סק) has been identified, though somewhat hesitatingly, with *Kafr Sa*, about 14 miles to the west of *Nâblus*, as there are numerous cases of *ḳôph* falling in ancient names in Palestine. As Saḳ, however, is included with Ḳeṣeh, Azzah, and Ḥaṣerot in the prefecture of the same steward (Gaddiyo), it was more probably in the immediate neighbourhood of these places, *i.e.* between Samaria and *Nâblus*.

Shereḳ (assuming its transliteration to be correct) might be *esh-Sherkie*, about 6 miles west of *'Arrâbeh*, or it might correspond with *Serkiteh*, the ruins of a village mentioned (according to Dussaud) on the French military map, about 7 miles south-west of *Nâblus*. 'Shereḳ,' however, is a very doubtful reading. The name occurs only on two *ostraka* (Nos. 42 and 48), on each of which it is partly obliterated. On the former the final letter bears more resemblance to *rêsh* than to *ḳôph*. In this case the name may be transliterated Seror, and can be identified almost certainly with *Deir Serûr*, 5 miles west of Samaria.

Shiphtan (or Shaphtan) may be *Shûfeh*, 7 miles west of Samaria, or *Jin-ṣâfût*,[1] 8 miles south-west of *Nâblus*.

Tetel, which occurs on *ostraka* Nos. 13 and 21, is evidently not the same as Ha-Tell. Dussaud has suggested *Kefr Thilth* (Baal-Shalisha), about 13 miles

[1] Cf. Robinson, *Palæstina*, iii. p. 887.

south-west of *Nâblus*, but the resemblance between the two names is rather fanciful. Tetel does not seem to correspond to any known place at the present day.

Yasheb, as Reisner vocalizes it, is probably the Biblical name Jashub (Nu 26^{24}), and may be found at *Yâsûf* (En-Tappuah), about 8 miles south of *Nâblus*. This is a very ancient village, partly in ruins, with a necropolis adjoining which bears evidences of the antiquity of the place.[1]

Yaṣit, which Reisner makes Yaṣot, is doubtless *Yaṣîd*, 5 miles north-east of Samaria, the Yusita of the Egyptian lists.[2]

While discussing the various places within the northern kingdom of Israel, it may not be out of place to refer to the vexed question of the location of Yenô'am (Egyptian, Yanu'am(u); Amarna Letters, Yanuama), which some scholars have placed at modern *Yânûḥ* near Tyre, others at *Hunîn*, about 10 miles north-west-by-north of Lake *Ḥûleh*, while others again, such as Dussaud, have identified it with the Biblical Yanôaḥ (Jos $16^{6.7}$, יָנוֹחָה, modern *Yânûn*) to the south-east of *Nâblus*. The name occurs under Thutmose III., and frequently in the Egyptian records of the XIXth Dynasty, but its occurrence on a stele of Seti I., discovered by Clarence S. Fisher at Beth-shean in 1922, raises the whole question in a new form. The stele describes the disposition of Seti's forces in their campaign in

[1] Guérin, *Samarie*, ii. p. 162. [2] Cf. Gautier, *Dict. Géogr.*, p. 48.

support of the chief of Beth-shean against a hostile league composed of the 'vile one' of Ḥamath and the men of Paḥira. These enemies had imprisoned the chief of Raḥubu in his city, and were evidently threatening Beth-shean. Seti divided his forces: the division of Ra was sent to occupy Beth-shean, that of Amūn proceeded against Ḥamath, and that of Sutekh ultimately marched to Yenô'am. Of the five places here referred to (Beth-shean, Ḥamath, Paḥira, Raḥubu, Yenô'am), the first four are not difficult to locate. Beth-shean is the modern *Beisân*; Ḥamath, where the revolt seems to have had its origin, is believed by most scholars to be *Tell el-Ḥammeh* (Amatha) at the entrance of the Yarmuk Pass just south of Tiberias;[1] Paḥira is Pella (modern *Tabakât Fâhil*), a city just across the Jordan from Beth-shean; and Raḥubu (or Rehob) is *Sheikh Riḥâb* (*Tell eṣ-Ṣarem*), a few miles to the south of Beth-shean. Professor Alexandre Moret would place Raḥubu in the neighbourhood of Acre on the Phœnician coast,[2] but in such a case how could it be besieged by the insurgents of Pella, at a time too when Megiddo and the whole plain of Esdraelon was in the hands of the Egyptians? And how, within such a wide stretch of country, could it be possible to say, as the text does, that the enemy succumbed at all points 'in a single day'? The

[1] Albright would prefer to locate it at *Tell el-Ḥammeh,* about 8 miles south on the road from *Beisân,* but this does not affect our point (cf. Albright, *Bull. American Schools,* No. 19, Oct. 1925, p. 18).

[2] *Revue de l'Egypt ancienne,* i. p. 18.

only likely location of Raḥubu is at *Sheikh Riḥâb.* In the Papyrus Anastasi I., the *maher* says, 'Pray teach me about K-y-n [modern *Ka'ûn*, about 6 miles south of *Beisân*], Rehob, Beth-shean, and Tarakael [modern *Zerra'a*, about 5 miles south of *Beisân*], the stream of Jordan, how it is crossed.' [1] The mention of these places together in one sentence is corroboration that Rehob must be near *Beisân*, and not away near the coast. According to the plan of campaign, Seti's troops marched from Megiddo to the east along the plain of Esdraelon and the valley of *Jâlûd*. While one column assisted the garrison at Beth-shean, and the second occupied the Ḥamath Pass, the third crossed the Jordan and seized Pella. The enemy, being attacked on all points at the same time, gave way, and the Egyptian forces, having regrouped themselves, pursued them northward in the direction of Damascus. It was on this occasion that Seti erected a tablet of victory at *esh-Shihâb*, in the Decapolis. His forces then marched on to Yenô'am, and this is the only town whose location is not so clearly revealed as the others. There is no Biblical town of this name, so famous in Egyptian records, where it is pictured as a *migdol* surrounded by trees (*i.e.* a forest-girt town), and with a small lake at its base.[2] But there is little difficulty in showing that it is identical with the Yanôaḥ (יָנוֹחַ) mentioned in 2 K 15[29], and must be placed a few

[1] *Cambridge Ancient History*, iii. p. 326.
[2] Cf. Müller, *Asien und Europa*, fig., p. 420.

miles north of Ḳadesh.[1] In the verse referred to we have the victorious march of Tiglath-pileser III. described. The Assyrian monarch marched down from the *Beḳâʿ* along the valley of the *Hâṣbâny*, capturing on the way ʿIyôn (=*el-Khiam*, in *Merj ʿAyûn*, about 16 miles north of Lake *Ḥûleh*), Abel Beth-Maʿakah (=*Âbl*, 5 miles south of ʿIyôn), Yanôaḥ (יָנוֹחַ=?), Ḳadesh (=*Ḳades Naphtali*, 10½ miles south of *Âbl*), and Ḥaṣor (=*el-Kedah*, the Hazura of the Tell el-Amarna Letters, about 3½ miles south-west of Lake *Ḥuleh*),[2] followed by Gilead, Galilee, and all the land of Naphtali.[3] A reference to the map shows that these places are mentioned in order of march from north to south,[4] but there is no name of any place corresponding to 'Yanôaḥ' between Abel Beth-Maʿakah and Ḳadesh. Almost midway, however (and a trifle eastward), between the two places we find *Tell en-Nâʿameh*, which occupies a strong position covering the entrance of the Jordan Valley in the region just north of Lake *Ḥûleh* immediately beyond the marshes.[5] This name has been

[1] Cf. Albright, *Bull. American Schools*, No. 19, Oct. 1925, pp. 12 ff.

[2] We are indebted to Professor J. Garstang for identifying Ḥaṣor with *el-Kedah*. Cf. *Annals of Archæology and Anthropology*, xiv. Nos. 1 and 2.

[3] Cf. a similar enumeration in 1 K 15[20], where Ben-hadad's armies are said to have smitten ʿIyôn, Dan (=*Tell el-Kâdy*, 4 miles east of *Âbl*), and Abel Beth-Maʿakah, with all Chinneroth and the land of Naphtali.

[4] Cf. *Atlas of the Historical Geography of the Holy Land.*

[5] This site is not mentioned in the *Atlas of the Historical Geography*, but will be found on the British War Office map, No. 2321, Joppa-Damascus Sheet, Dec. 1916.

shown to be the exact equivalent in Arabic of the ancient Egypto-Assyrian Yanu'am.[1] We may thus conclude with some degree of certainty that Yenô'am (יְנוֹעַם) and the Biblical Yanôaḥ (יָנוֹחַ) are one and the same place, the former being the regular and more ancient (Canaanite) form, and the latter the Hebrew one, as Max Müller has suggested,[2] and that the place lies a few miles north of Kadesh Naphtali, and not near Tyre or at *Hunîn* or in the vicinity of *Nâblus*. The monument erected by Seti in the Decapolis shows that his forces advanced northward on the east side of the Jordan and not anywhere near Tyre, which was away from the sphere of rebellion; and those scholars who place Yenô'am near *Nâblus* find it necessary to postulate two Egyptian towns of the former name (as Dussaud does), one in the north and the other in the south, which seems rather unlikely.

[1] H. Clauss, *Zeitschrift des deutschen Palästina-Vereins*, xxx., 1907, pp. 34 f.; Albright, *Bull. American Schools*, No. 19, Oct. 1925, pp. 12 f.

[2] *Asien und Europa*, p. 394.

CHAPTER V

THE ADMINISTRATIVE SYSTEM

THE *ostraka*, as already stated, contain notes or accounts of oil and wine received at the palace store by the governors or stewards. That they were connected with the royal household is evident from the fact that they were found in a building adjoining the palace and are dated according to the years of reign. The reading on some of them, after the lapse of about twenty-eight centuries, is of course imperfect and doubtful, on others it is incomplete owing to breakage, and on many it is quite illegible, but over sixty of them have yielded satisfactory results. According to Reisner, they are really accompanying notes (similar to way-bills) sent with the oil or wine for entry in the accounts, and they naturally mention only the bare essentials.[1] Thus, *ostrakon* No. 1 (from a fragment of a flaring bowl of reddish-brown ware, broken in two) says: '*In the tenth year* [*sent*] *to Shemaryo from* [*the town of*] *Be'er-yam jar*[*s ?*] *of old* [*wine*], [*viz.*] *Rage*ʿ [*son of*][2] *Elisha*ʿ . . . 2, ʿ*Uzza*

[1] For specimens of the *ostraka*, see p. 40, where Nos. 1, 13, 17, and 19 are given.

[2] The expression 'son of' is omitted on the *ostraka*, as generally on ancient Israelite seals and in modern Arabic.

[*son of*] . . . 1, *Eliba* [*son of*] . . . 1, *Ba'ala* [*son of*] *Elisha'* . . . 1, *Yeda'yo* [*son of*] . . . 1.' This means that Shemaryo, a royal steward, received contributions of wine from the town of Be'er-yam, and the names of the consigners are added, with the number of jars that each furnished. This is the interpretation put on this and similar inscriptions by Père Vincent and other scholars, and is doubtless correct.[1] The word used for 'year' is שת (instead of שנת), as in the Moabite inscription and the Neo-Punic ones. Again, No. 13 (from a jar of grey ware baked pinkish-buff), as deciphered by Albright and Dussaud, says: '*In the year* 10 [*sent*] *from* [*the town of*] *Abi'ezer to Shemaryo a jar of old wine* [נבל ין ישן]. *To Isha* [*a jar of old wine*] *from* [*the town of*] *Tetel.*' Here Shemaryo and Isha (probably hypocoristic for Ish-Ba'al) are the names of royal stewards. The expression 'old wine' corresponds to the Septuagint reading of Am 6[6], 'pure clarified wine' (the only rendering that gives sense).[2] Accordint to the *ostraka*, there seems to have been no lack of vineyards within the Israelite territory (cf. Dt 8[8]). Most of them were probably on hillsides or stony slopes, which were dug in terrace fashion to prevent the thin layer of soil from being washed away in winter. Sometimes the vine-stems were trained to grow tall, but usually they were allowed to trail on the surface of the soil, and the cluster-bearing

[1] Cf. *Revue biblique*, 1925, p. 440, note 3.

[2] Cf. Dussaud, *Samarie au temps d'Achab*, 1926, i. p. 25, note 2.

branches were propped up by forked sticks. They were pruned at the end of the fruiting season, so that in winter the plants were reduced to their trunks and a few principal branches. It was chiefly red grapes that were grown (Gn 49^{11}, Dt 32^{14}, Pr 23^{31}), and the size of them may be gathered from the report of the spies (Nu $13^{23ff.}$), although this was no doubt exaggerated. The pride which the Israelite husbandman had in his vineyard finds expression in Naboth's words to Ahab, 'The Lord forbid it me that I should give the inheritance of my fathers to thee.' A third example, No. 17 (from a similar piece of grey ware), reads as follows: '*In the year* 10 [*sent*] *from Azzah to Gaddiyo a jar of fine oil* [נבל שמן רחץ].' A fourth example, No. 19 (written on a similar fragment), says: '*In the year* 10 *from* [*the town of*] *Yaṣit a jar of fine oil* [נבל שמן רחץ] *to Ahino'am.*' In the two latter cases שמן רחץ probably means oil for anointing the body, corresponding to רֵאשִׁית שְׁמָנִים, 'choice oil,' which was used for this purpose (Am 6^{6}). The regions around Samaria were noted for the purity of the oil which they produced. The secret of its purity evidently lay in the people gathering the olives direct from the trees, while in other cases, such as near the coast, where there was less time for this kind of work, they waited till the fruit fell to the ground. Josephus tells us that when he was governor of Galilee vast sums of money were made by John of Gischala through selling the pure oil of Galilee (ἔλαιον καθαρόν, corresponding to the שמן רחץ of the *ostraka*) to the Jews at Cæsarea and the coast, who could not secure such oil there and would not be dependent on the Greeks.[1]

It was Solomon who first introduced an organized system of royal stewards, and the kings of Israel seem to have continued it or copied it.[2] The *ostraka* confirm the historical accuracy of 1 K 4^{7-19}, where we are informed that the upkeep of Solomon's house, his personnel, and his cavalry was attended to by twelve district stewards (נִצָּבִים), whose names are given,[3] each of whom took his turn for a month at a time, securing the necessary supplies from a district allocated to him. These stewards or administrative officers of Solomon do not seem to have displaced the tribal chiefs, for the old tribal boundaries of the Book of Joshua (which had been

[1] Josephus, *Life*, 13.

[2] R. P. Dougherty ('Cuneiform Parallels, etc.,' in *Annual, Amer. Schools*, 1923–4) has tried to show that a similar organization of royal stewards under a special officer 'in charge of the royal basket' is found in the cuneiform texts of the Neo-Babylonian period (*c.* sixth century B.C.). But the purpose of this arrangement seems to have been to gather the taxes and offerings for the temples, and bears no intrinsic resemblance to Solomon's idea.

[3] In 1 K $4^{8ff.}$. It is supposed by some that, in vv.$^{8-14}$, the names of the stewards have lapsed, so that Ben- ('son of') only remains, probably owing to the incorporated document being an ancient one and rather imperfect. The lapse would be accounted for if the upper right-hand corner of the original papyrus sheet had been injured or broken off. The document, being an important administrative one, had probably been copied often, and must have been in a corrupt state before falling into the hands of the redactor. At the same time this explanation of the omission of the names is perhaps unnecessary, for the patronymic alone was occasionally written, perhaps for brevity's sake, as in the Bethphage lists (cf. *Syria*, 1923, p. 245), and is common among the Arabs.

taken probably from ancient sources by the priestly compiler) continued down to the time of David and Solomon, though they gradually ceased to be political divisions. The order of the names is not strictly geographical, nor do the districts correspond, except roughly, with the tribal territories. The order is probably that of the months for which the stewards were severally responsible, and the districts were marked out according to the capabilities of the country. The stewards were merely purveyors or providers for the king, his *annonæ curatores.*[1] The daily consumption was enormous (1 K $4^{22.\ 23}$), comprising 30 *cor* of fine flour, 60 *cor* of meal, 10 fat oxen, 20 oxen out of the pastures, and 100 sheep, without reckoning the harts, gazelles, roebucks, and fatted fowl. But the supplies were not all required for Jerusalem: there were chariot and cavalry centres outside the capital (1 K 10^{26}), for accommodation had to be found for 1400 chariots, 4000 horses,[2] and 12,000 horsemen. Some of the supplies too, such as barley and straw destined for the horses and swift steeds, were brought to the place where the king happened to be (1 K 4^{28}).

The arrangements in the northern kingdom were probably a continuation of those in Solomon's time. We read, for instance, of Obadiah, one of Ahab's

[1] For a treatment of this subject see Alt, *Alttestamentliche Studien Rudolph Kittel*, Leipzig, 1913, pp. 1–19; Albright, *Journ. of Pal. Orient. Soc.*, v. (1925), i. pp. 17 ff. The writer feels indebted to the latter for many suggestions.

[2] According to 2 Ch 9^{25}, instead of 40,000 as in 1 K 4^{26}.

stewards, searching during the famine for grass to keep the king's horses and mules alive, and on another occasion feeding a hundred prophets, which he no doubt did, not from mere religious sentiments, but because he regarded it as part of his duty, seeing that they belonged to the king's establishment. It is also recorded that Elah, who was King of Israel twelve years before Ahab, was assassinated by Zimri, a cavalry officer, while he was intoxicated in the house of his steward, which goes to show that the latter had charge of the contributions of wine. According to the Biblical account, therefore, the system of stewards that existed in Solomon's time seems to have continued in the northern kingdom after the disruption. The probability is that only one of Solomon's twelve districts (1 K 4^{7-19}), namely, that of Judah (v.^{19b}, 'and a steward who was in the land of Judah')[1] remained loyal to the southern kingdom,[2] and the remaining eleven attached themselves to the northern. These eleven appear to have been as follows, judging from the passage in 1 K $4^{8ff.}$:[3]

[1] By connecting the word Judah of v.^{20} to the end of v.^{19}. It may be possible that one 'Judah' has been lost by haplography.

[2] Simeon at the time of the disruption seems to have had no independent existence, having been practically absorbed by Judah.

[3] This old document, to which we have already referred, shows signs of having originated in the northern kingdom, for it puts Ephraim at the head of the list and only mentions the district of Judah briefly at the end. It is true, it states that two of the stewards (those over Dôr and Naphtali) married daughters of Solomon, but this statement may have been made for political reasons (cf. Albright, *Journ. of Pal. Orient. Soc.*, v. (1925), p. 36).

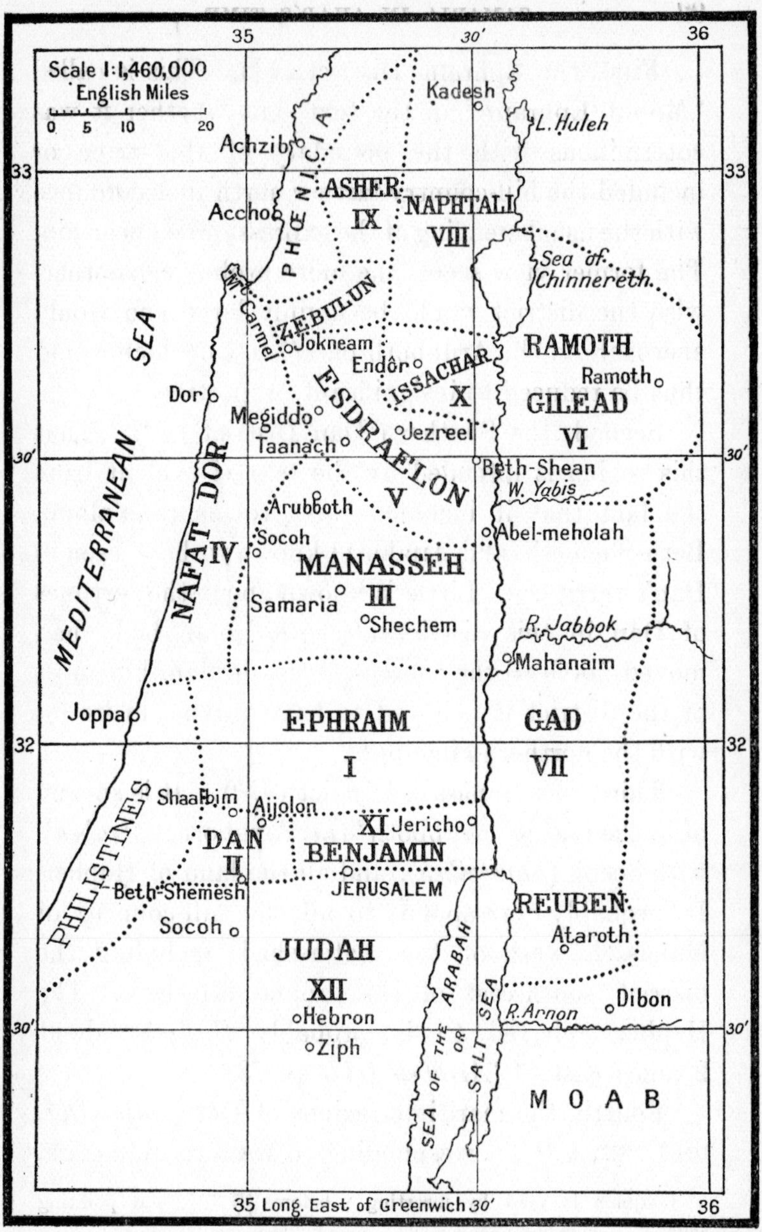

Map of Israel's Administrative Districts

First, the Ephraim District (v.[8]). This is called 'Mount Ephraim' in the text, but whether it was coterminous with the boundary of this tribe or included the hill-country farther north in accordance with the usual meaning of the expression, is uncertain. The former view seems the more probable, as otherwise the district would be unduly large and would encroach on the Arubboth one (No. 3), which would thus be reduced to insignificant proportions.

Second, the Southern Dan District (v.[9]). That this region is intended by the text is evident from the fact that it included three towns (Sha'albîm, Beth-Shemesh, and Aijalon)[1] known to have been in Dan's territory. Little is known about the fortunes of Dan in this district after the main body had moved north to the sources of the Jordan, but most of the district is believed to have thrown in its lot with the northern kingdom.

Third, the Manasseh District (v.[10]). It is spoken of in the text as 'Arubboth' (*i.e.* Arruboth, '*Arrâbeh*), with Socoh (*Shuweikeh*), and all the land of Ḥepher. It probably corresponds to all the hill-country of Manasseh west of the water-shed, including the district south-east of this, round Shechem. The Ḥepher referred to is probably *Ḥafireh*, about 2 miles east of '*Arrâbeh* (*vide* p. 73).

Fourth, the maritime regions of Dôr (*Nāfat Dôr*, נָפַת דּאֹר, v.[11]), corresponding to western Manasseh.

[1] Aijalon is read by inserting ו before בֵּית חָנָן, and pointing אילון absolute (אַיָּלוֹן) instead of construct (אֵילוֹן).

Dôr (Egyptian *Dr*, Assyrian *Du'ru*, Hellenic *Dora*) has been identified with *Ṭanṭûrah*, on the coast, 9 Roman miles north of Cæsarea.[1] The term *nāfat*, *nāfā*, is generally understood as 'height,' but the meaning intended is probably 'coast region' or 'maritime region' (ἡ παραλία, as Symmachus renders the term), from the idea 'cliff,' 'precipice.'[2] The probability is that *nāfat* was prefixed to distinguish the coast Dôr from 'Endôr (*'En-dôr*, 'fountain of Dor'), just north of the plain of Esdraelon, with which it was apt to be confused (cf. Jos 12^{23} 11^{2}). This administrative district, therefore, would likely include the territory from Carmel to near Joppa, with Dôr as the chief town.

Fifth, the Esdraelon District (v.^{12}). This extended from beyond Jokneam, in the extreme north-western end of the plain of Esdraelon, through the entire length of the plain to Beth-shean, and down the Jordan valley to the region of Abel-meḥolah (*'Ain Ḥelweh*). The text reads, 'Taanach and Megiddo, all Beth-shean (which is beside Zarethan beneath Jezreel), from Beth-shean to Abel-meḥolah (and away north-west) as far as beyond Jokneam.' The last clause should have stood at the beginning,

[1] Cf. Lagarde, *Onomasticon Sacra*, 115 (2nd ed., 149); Wilson, *Lands of the Bible*, ii. p. 249; van de Velde, *Narrative of a Journey through Syria and Palestine*, i. p. 333; Baedeker, *Palestine*, p. 238. Phythian-Adams, while identifying the extra-Biblical Dôr with *Ṭanṭûrah*, is inclined to fix the Biblical one at *Tell el-Makerkush*, on the *Wady Sherrar*, near the Jordan (cf. *P.E.F. Quarterly*, Jan. 1929, p. 61). But such a location places this administrative district within the heart of another, and cannot therefore be correct.

[2] Cf. Dahl, *Materials for the History of Dor*, pp. 21–27.

but it had evidently been omitted there, and was inserted at the end. The southern boundary of this district must have extended south of the great plain, seeing that it included Taanach. Probably it included also the whole of the Gilboa region. The district thus corresponded roughly to northern and eastern Manasseh west of the Jordan (cf. Jos 17^{4}), and the administrative capital was probably Megiddo, which was the largest town in the district.

Sixth, the Ramoth-Gilead District, on the east of the Jordan, including the half-tribe of Manasseh. The text here is a doublet, consisting of vv.$^{13. 19.}$ It has generally been supposed that two different districts are referred to, but a comparison of the two verses shows that they refer to one and the same. The second verse had probably been a marginal variant, and had afterwards crept into the text at the end of the list. The description is a little mixed owing to narratives introduced by the Deuteronomic redactors (cf. Dt 3^{4}, etc.), but the district included the towns of Jair (חַוֹּת יָאִיר; cf. also Dt 3^{14}, Jos 13^{30}, Jg 10^{4}, 1 Ch 2^{23}) and the region of Argob, although its boundaries on the east must have been very vague and have varied from reign to reign. The capital would doubtless be at Ramoth-Gilead, believed to be modern *er-Remṭeh*, in the north-eastern corner of Gilead, about 32 miles east of Beth-shean.

Seventh, the Maḥanaim District (v.^{14}), corresponding to southern Gilead, and including the tribal divisions of Gad and Reuben. Maḥanaim has been variously located, but the most probable site appears to be *Tulûl ed-Dahab*, about 7 miles east of Jordan, in a bend of the *Nahr ez-Zerka* (Jabbok). It was David's capital during Absalom's revolt, and thus came to be a place of much importance in southern Gilead. How far south this district extended we cannot tell. In Omri's time, according to Mesha's stele, it may have reached to ʿAṭaroth and perhaps the Arnon. The dividing line between the preceding district and this one may have been the *Wâdy Yâbis*, about midway between the respective capitals.

Eighth, the Naphtali District (v.[15]), which contained some of the finest territory in the kingdom, rich and beautifully diversified, with an abundance of olive trees and vineyards. It included the lofty region to the north-west of the Sea of Chinnereth, as well as the plain of ʿIyôn (*Merj ʿAyûn*) in the valley west of Hermon. The boundaries cannot be fixed with certainty, but in Omri's time the district extended probably as far as the land lying around the springs of Jordan.

Ninth, the Asher and Zebulun District (v.[16]). The text reads 'Asher and Beʿaloth.' The latter name is unknown, except as that of a town in the extreme south of Judah (Jos 15[24]), and Albright would transfer it to the next district in place of Issachar, and would make it correspond with the Beʿaloth to which we have just referred.[1] But there

[1] *Journal of the Pal. Orient. Soc.*, v. (1925), p. 35.

seems no need for such a radical alteration of the passage. The words 'and Be'aloth' in the Hebrew (ובעלות) are apparently a corruption for Zebulun (זבולון), as half of the Hebrew letters are identical and the others are liable to be confused in the ancient scripts, and Zebulun was a small tribe adjoining Asher on the south. The corruption may also be suspected from the fact that otherwise Zebulun would have no place whatever in the list.

Tenth, the Issachar District. This may seem a small one, but it must be remembered that our knowledge of this tribe is meagre, for the delimitation of its boundaries in Jos 19^{17-23} is from the hands of the Priestly redactor.[1] It lay south of Zebulun and Naphtali, and north of Manasseh; and as the administrative districts allocated to the stewards did not correspond fully with the tribal districts, it is possible that this one included part of Naphtali (No. 8). The administrative capital may have been at 'Endôr, already an important and ancient town in those days, which figures in the lists of Thutmose III. about 1480 B.C.

Eleventh, the Benjamin District (v.^{18}). According to a passage in Joshua (18^{11-28}), this tribe possessed twenty-six towns, but it is very doubtful whether it could call all these its own. The question has been discussed as to whether Benjamin actually

[1] Cf. Moore on Jg 5^{15}. For Issachar's limits, see *The Boundary between Issachar and Naphtali*, by Aapeli Saarisalo (Suomalaisen Tiedeakatemian Toimituksia, Helsinki, 1927); Albright, 'The Topography of the Tribe of Issachar,' in *Zeit. für die Alttest. Wissen.*, 1926, pp. 225 f.

threw in its lot with the northern kingdom. According to some passages it remained with Judah, but according to others with Israel. Thus, we read 'there was none that followed the house of David but the tribe of Judah only' (1 K 12^{20}). The truth probably is that most of Benjamin, especially the northern part of it, joined the revolt, and would thus form an administrative district under the northern kingdom.

These eleven districts, as already stated, would probably be preserved with few changes, if any, by Jeroboam I. and his successors. Some of them had to be left doubtless to neighbouring enemies in the course of a few generations, or at least suffered considerable decrease. The Aramæans on the north-east, the Moabites, and ultimately the Assyrians left Israel with very little territory, if any, on the east of Jordan. The Israel that succumbed in 722 B.C. was very much smaller than when Jeroboam I. began to reign.

The taxes in wine and oil from each district would be collected at the capital or principal town of the district and dispatched to the royal residence or to the place arranged by the central authorities. After Samaria was built, this city would naturally be not only the capital of the land, but also the administrative centre, instead of Arubboth, for the Manasseh District. It is evident that the *ostraka* are connected with oil and wine received from this district alone, seeing that the towns mentioned are all within it, and the *ostraka* were all found in the storerooms of Ahab's palace. It follows that the stewards mentioned are deputy ones, each of whom looked after a sub-district or prefecture. It was their special business to gather the royal revenues from the estates or towns within their own prefecture, and to deliver them at the palace store in Samaria with an accompanying note for entry in the accounts, so that the contributions could be credited to the senders. The characteristic formula on the *ostraka* runs thus: 'In the . . . year. Sent from (a place) to (a person). A jar of wine (or oil). To be credited to (a second person or persons).'

The inscriptions, which thus seem to be in accord with the arrangements referred to in the Biblical history, give us the names of royal deputy-stewards or recipients (the consignees), the districts under their charge, the consignments of wine and oil received, and in many cases the names of the consigners. Unfortunately, we do not have the names of all the deputy-stewards for any one year, but the names of over a dozen altogether are mentioned. They are as follows:

Aḥima (אחמא), Aḥino'am (אחנעם), Ba'alzamar (בעלזמר), Bedyo (?) (בדיו, =Biblical Bedeiah),[1]

[1] Such names on the *ostraka* end in יו, instead of the Biblical יָהוּ or יָה. The variation, as S. R. Driver has shown (*Old Testament Essays*, Griffin & Co., London, 1928), was purely 'a matter of fashion,' but whether the pronunciation was in all cases Yâ, as he thinks, is doubtful. The termination certainly means 'Yahweh'

Gaddiyo (גדיו, =Biblical Gaddiah or Gaddiel), Gamar (גמר, =Biblical Gomer), Ḥanan (son of) Ba'ara (חנן בערא), Ḥannino'(am) (חננע[ם]), Ḥeleṣ (son of) Gaddiyo (חלץ גדיו), Ḥeleṣ (son of) Afṣaḥ (חלץ אפצח), Isha (son of) Aḥimelek (אשא אחמלך), Nimshi (נמש[י]), Shemaryo (שמריו, =Biblical Shemariah), Yeda'yo (ידעיו, =Biblical Jedaiah). All of these, except Aḥima, Ba'alzamar, and Ḥannino'am, are Biblical names, and Ba'alzamar is a known Phœnician name.

Each of these deputy-stewards, as already stated, had charge of a certain area or prefecture within the Manasseh District. It is possible, indeed, to mark out the prefectures of some of them on the map. Thus, Gaddiyo, who received consignments from Ḳeṣeh, Azzah, Ḥaṣerot, and Saḳ, must have had charge of the area between Samaria and Shechem; Shemaryo, who received contributions from Abi'ezer, Etpar'an, Ha-Tell, and Be'er-yam, seems to have operated on the territory immediately north-west of Samaria; Aḥino'am, to whom Geba' and Yaṣit

in the Israelite names. It is well to understand, however, that the tetragrammaton does not occur in the documents of the Ist Dynasty at Babylon (*c.* 2169–1870 B.C.), as some scholars suggest. The names *Yawi-ilum*, etc., discussed by Delitzsch, consist of the west Semitic verb *awu* (=Babylonian *emu*, or the like, in such names as *Ime-Shamash*), meaning 'to utter,' used in the 3rd pers. sing.+*ilum* (cf. Schorr, *Urkunden des Altbabylonischen Zivil und Prozessrechts*, No. 210, note on 4). Nor does there seem to be any proof of a Yahweh prefix in the name *Yaubi'di* (king of Hamath, *c.* 720 B.C.), which is also written *Ilu-Yaubi'di*, and means 'God (*ilu*) uttereth my rest' (cf. west Semitic name *Yaḳba-bieda*, 'he speaketh rest'). The explanation of such names by German scholars has been somewhat *risqué* (cf. Sidney Smith, *Cambridge Ancient History*, iii. p. 57 n.).

sent their contributions, evidently had control of the places adjoining Samaria on the north-east. The material at our disposal in the *ostraka* is unfortunately too limited to enable us to allocate all the prefectures, and thus give a complete picture of the fiscal organization, but it is clear that there was a well-arranged system for gathering in the royal revenues.

Among the senders of contributions there are also many with Biblical names: ʻAbedyo (עבדיו = Obadiah) son of Abiyo (אביו = Abiah, Abijah),[1] Aḥaz (אחז), Aḥzai (אחזי), ʻAlah son of Ela (עלה אלא), Elishaʻ (אלישע), Gera son of Yo-yosheb (גרא יויושב), Gera son of Ḥanni'ab (גרא חנאב), Isha son of Baʻalʻazkar (אשא בעלעזכר), [Ḳ]edar (קדר), Meribaʻal (מרבעל),[2] Rafa son of ʻAnimes (רפא ענמש), Shebaʻ (שבע), ʻUzza (עזא). The non-Biblical ones (not mentioning names which occur in the above list of stewards) are: Abibaʻal (אבבעל), Baʻala son of Elishaʻ (בעלא אלישע), Baʻala son of Zakar (בעלא זכר), Baʻala son of Baʻalmeʻoni (בעלא בעלמעני), Eliba (?) (אלבא), Marnayo son of Natan (מרניו נתן), Marnayo son of Gaddiyo (מרניו גדיו), Rageʻ son of Elishaʻ (רגע אלישע), Yeʻush (יעש). Other names occurring, but which cannot be classed among those of either stewards or senders, are Aḥa the Judæan (אחא יהדי), ʻAbda (עבדא = Abda or

[1] 'Abiyo' is doubtful: the name may be read 'Ariyo.'

[2] Meribaʻal was the name of Jonathan's son, which the redactors changed to Mephibosheth.

Obadiah), ʿEgelyo (עגליו),[1] and Yo-yadaʿ (יוידע = Joiada, Jehoiada).

Judging from the numerous senders, the provisioning of Ahab's household, added to the cost of his superb 'ivory' palace, must have been a large burden on his subjects. With the help of Amos and contemporary history, we can picture the social life that went on, especially in the royal household and among the upper classes. The firm but despotic rule of Ahab, which maintained the military traditions of the house of Omri, led to increasing wealth and prosperity. There was great display of pomp and luxury, with many 'ivory' houses in imitation of Ahab's (cf. Am 3^{15}). New cities were founded, perhaps the result of the flourishing commerce with the coast. The material prosperity of the reign was almost as great as that of Solomon a century before. The indignant protest of Jeremiah to Jehoiachin (Jer 22^{15}, LXXA), 'Art thou a true king because thou viest with Ahab?' gives an insight into the grandeur. But all this was accompanied by injustice and moral corruption. Under the influence of Jezebel, who brought much pomp and prestige with her from Tyre, the halls of the extensive palace must have witnessed many a scene of luxury and extravagance.

Out of the above names, amounting to at least fifty-two, it is noteworthy that there are eleven, or about one-fifth of the number, which have *yah* as an

[1] For this name, see p. 145, note 1.

element. This does not, of course, prove anything as to the popularity or otherwise of Yahweh in Ahab's time, for the men bearing these names, being adults, must have received them some years before Ahab's succession. But it shows that Yahweh names had begun to flourish by the beginning of the ninth century. They had become to a large extent the style at that early period. Evidence proves that it was only about the time of David that such names came into vogue.[1] In the Book of Joshua there does not appear to be even one. In Judges there are but two, Joash and Micah, and the latter is doubtful.[2] In the Books of Samuel, though scores of names occur, there are not a dozen Yahweh ones, and in some of these the supposed Yahweh terminations may be merely hypocoristic.[3] Among the forty-three names of David's mighty men (2 S 23), only two (Benaiah and Jonathan) have a Yahweh element, and of the names of his seventeen or more sons, only three (including Jedidah, a name which Nathan gave to Solomon) are of this kind. In spite of all this, however, it is evident that the worship of Yahweh had made considerable advances in the northern kingdom before Ahab's time. If its centre or driving force was in the south, it had gradually succeeded in permeating the northern districts also. Probably it had received an impetus there from the

[1] Cf. G. Buchanan Gray, *Hebrew Proper Names* (1896), pp. 257 ff.

[2] Gray, *op cit.* p. 157.

[3] Cf. J. M. Powis Smith, *American Journal of Semitic Languages and Literatures*, 1918, p. 15, note 2.

prosperous and brilliant reign of Solomon, and it does not appear to have been retarded by the rupture between north and south (*c.* 937 B.C.) resulting in the formation of two independent and hostile kingdoms. Its progress must have been largely due to the courage and faith of the prophets. The task they had in the northern kingdom was far from easy, for there Baalism and other cults were deeply entrenched, and had behind them the sanction of centuries. The Israelites had come from the nomadic life of the desert into a heathenism that was already age-long. Yahwism had to be grafted upon the old stocks or planted in this arid soil. But the prophets succeeded, and though Baal worship was never by any means eradicated from the northern kingdom and a kind of syncretism existed for many centuries, the worship of Yahweh must have struck its roots deep there long before Ahab began to rule.

These arrangements for supplies to the king throw light on the problem of the jar-handles of the type 'for the king' (למלך) found in excavations in the south of Palestine. These stamps do not give the name of any personal consigner, but simply that of the administrative town or district, and they thus resemble *ostrakon* No. 63, which gives only the date and the name of the town, '*In the year* 17, *from Shemida*'.' They belong to a much later period than the *ostraka*, sometime probably between 750 and 600 B.C.,[1] but they evidently refer to the dues

[1] Cf. Vincent, *Canaan*, pp. 359 f.; Dussaud, *Syria* (1925), pp. 335,

furnished by certain centres of administration in Judah to the royal establishment at Jerusalem. There are four such centres mentioned—Hebron, Ziph, Socoh, and Memshath. It is possible, of course, that these towns may have been places of pottery manufacture for the king (cf. 1 Ch 4[23]), as Sayce, Clermont-Ganneau, Père Vincent, and Driver suggest.[1] But the handles show such identity of type and material that they could not possibly have come from different factories. According to Macalister, the clay and technique of the modern potteries at Ramleh, Jerusalem, Gaza, and other centres possess such criteria that the work of each town can easily be distinguished. In the case of these pre-exilic handles, however, they bear such a resemblance to each other, whatever town they are stamped with, that they might all have come from the same factory.[2] Indeed, it is not unlikely that they were all made by the potters resident at Neṭa'im, Gederah, and neighbouring villages (1 Ch 4[23], R.V.). If we are to judge from the Samaria *ostraka*, the probability therefore is that the four towns mentioned were administrative centres, 'centres of districts in which were collected the dues in kind of the surrounding villages,' [3] and the jars were intended and

337; Macalister, 'The Craftsmen's Guild of the Tribe of Judah,' in *P.E.F. Quarterly Statement*, 1905, pp. 243–253, 328–342; Albright, *Journ. of Palest. Orient. Soc.*, 1925, pp. 46 ff.

[1] Vincent, *Canaan*, pp. 358 ff.; Driver, *Schweich Lectures*, p. 76.

[2] Cf. Albright, *Journ. of Palest. Orient. Soc.*, 1925, p. 48.

[3] Macalister, *Excavations in Palestine*, p. 114. Macalister after-

used for the purpose of consigning wine, oil, and other products from various places to these centres and thence to the royal household. The fact that the jars are all so similar is due to their representing current measures of capacity (officially gauged), and thus facilitating the administrative work.

Jar-handles, bearing these stamps, were first discovered at Jerusalem during Warren's excavations, and since then they have turned up in numerous sites elsewhere, but only within the borders of pre-exilic Judah. In addition to Jerusalem, they have been found in Gezer,[1] Jericho,[2] Gibeah (*Tell el-Fûl*), Azekah (*Tell Zachariyeh*), Mareshah (*Tell Sandaḥanna*), and several other places. As considerably over a hundred have been found, and not one of them in Israelite or Philistine territory, it follows that they are essentially Judæan. The stamps, as such, no doubt reveal foreign influence, being either scarabs after the Egyptian custom, or winged sun-disks (or 'flying rolls,' cf. Zec 5^{1-4}) after the Assyro-Persian models; but the practice they apparently reveal of towns sending contributions to the king's household is quite Israelite, dating probably from the time of Solomon's administration.

wards abandoned this theory, but with insufficient reasons. The objections urged against it seem to the writer to have no weight.

[1] Macalister, *Gezer*, ii. pp. 209 f.

[2] Sellin, *Jericho*, p. 158.

CHAPTER VI

AHAB'S FOREIGN POLICY

THE age in which Ahab lived was a stirring one, full of great dynastic changes. His foreign policy was affected thereby, for Israel was inextricably interwoven, both geographically and historically, with other nations to the north and east, such as Phœnicia, Damascus, and Assyria. There was an intermingling of the most varied political influences. Many of his actions, together with the causes of the Aramæan-Israelite and other wars, cannot be understood without an accurate conception of the international situation. It is here that many Biblical critics have erred.

Unfortunately, the dynasty of Omri and Ahab has been placed in an unfavourable light by the editors of 1 and 2 Kings, who have viewed the northern kingdom with a narrow, restricted, Judæan outlook. But though the dynasty lasted only about fifty years, it occupies a large space in the Biblical record, and contemporary history shows it to have been more important than the editors allow. After the disruption of the powerful Davidic monarchy, Samaria, rather than Jerusalem, became the centre of Israel's life. For several generations the northern kingdom was the predominant partner, possessing as it did the greater territory, and including the larger, richer, and more vital section of the people. Not only did it have the ascendancy over Judah, but its conquests east of the Jordan resulted in the subjection of Moab, and the payment by King Mesha, a wealthy sheep-owner, of a heavy tribute of wool. The enactments of Omri and Ahab became traditional, being referred to by the prophet Micah a century and a half later (Mic 6^{16}), and for many ages the Assyrians continued to call Israel *Bît-Ḫumrî* ('the House of Omri').[1] It is clear that Ahab, in addition to building a number of cities and a superb royal residence, was a successful statesman and intrepid warrior. The forces which he was able to put into the battle of Ḳarḳar (2000 chariots and 10,000 infantry) are probably exaggerated, but they show the relative position of his kingdom among neighbouring ones. It was small certainly, almost insignificant as compared with Egypt or Assyria, and probably less powerful than Damascus, but it held high rank throughout Palestine and Syria. One has only to remember that the Biblical record is artificial, having been edited from the special standpoint of a later age (*c.* 600 B.C.),

[1] Rawlinson, *Cuneiform Inscriptions of Western Asia*, iii. 10, 2, l. 17 f.; Schrader, *Die Keilinschriften und das Alte Testament*, 3rd ed., 1903, p. 265. Similarly, '*Mâr-Ḫumrî*' is 'son of *Ḫumrî*' (cf. Shalmaneser's inscription on his Black Obelisk, where Jehu is so described).

long after the northern kingdom had disappeared (722 B.C.) and when the Judæan monarchy alone survived. The whole record, indeed, has been through the hands of later editors from the south, who naturally regarded the northern tribes as schismatic and faithless to Yahweh, while they pictured Judah alone as true. The result is that we have a Judaic estimate of Ahab, very imperfect and one-sided. To obtain a correct view we have to make considerable allowances in the narrative. It is only because the editors have not carried through their task to perfection in every small detail, and because contemporary history comes to our assistance, that we are able to paint Ahab's life in less sombre colours.

Omri and Ahab probably adopted a wise policy in maintaining a close alliance with Phœnicia, which extended along the coast from Mount Carmel as far north as Aradus or Arvad (a stretch of about 200 miles), and inland as far as the Lebanon range, and was rising at this time into renewed activity as a maritime and commercial power. About a century before Ahab's time, Solomon had established a treaty with Hiram I. of Tyre (cf. Am 1^{9}), and owned with him a 'Tarshish' fleet (1 K 10^{22}), which apparently went to Tartessus in Spain and other distant places.[1] Omri and Ahab continued

[1] The term 'Tarshish' has no connection with Tarsus in Cilicia, but is a corruption of Tartessus. It has now been found in one of Esarhaddon's texts (*c.* 681 B.C.): *Tar-ši-ši* (and not *Nu-ši-ši*); cf. *Revue biblique*, 1927, p. 105. The term came to be vaguely used as

this friendly relationship, and the latter cemented it by taking as wife Jezebel, daughter of Ithobaal (' Baal is with him '), the Sidonian priest-king, who had gained the throne by the assassination of Phelles. Ithobaal ruled all Phœnicia, and is credited by later writers with the foundation of Botrys (north of Byblus) and Auza (in Libya).[1] The same year that Ahab began to rule in Israel, Baal-azar II., a brother of Jezebel, ascended the Phœnician throne, followed six years later by Mattan-baal, her nephew. The alliance between the two kingdoms was thus very close. Whatever may be said of it religiously, it was of much importance politically and commercially, for it gave the Israelites not only an ally to the north but convenient markets and seaports for their trade. Like the ' Canaanites,' they were ' traffickers ' (cf. Hos 12^7), though they probably had no trading vessels on the Mediterranean. The only port in Israelite territory, Joppa, had a very bad roadstead and harbour. It is never mentioned by pre-exilic writers, and it is questionable if the Israelites ever occupied it. On the other hand, the amount of trade that went out from Phœnicia

signifying the countries to the extreme west of the Mediterranean, and the expression ' ships of Tarshish ' came to denote merely a certain type of ships adapted for long journeys (cf. our ' East Indiamen '). In 1914, Dr. S. Contenau discovered a sarcophagus at Sidon bearing a representation of a Phœnician merchant vessel, evidently a ' ship of Tarshish ' (*La Civilization phénicienne* (1926), pp. 23, 297).

[1] He is called King of Sidon in 1 K 16^{31}, but he was more than this (cf. Menander, in Josephus, *Antiq.* VIII. xiii. 1). Sidon held sway over the other Phœnician cities.

by caravan or through its seaports cannot be measured. Of Phœnician goods alone, fine coloured glass, jewels, perfumes, purple cloth (of which the Phœnicians had the monopoly), embroidery, artistic bronze cups, and many other articles were taken by caravan to Mesopotamia, Asia Minor, and Egypt, or were shipped to distant colonies.[1] In addition, the corn, wine, fine oil, preserved fruits, dressed skins, honey, balsam, and other products of Israel found a ready market in Tyre and Sidon, to remain there or be carried with Phœnician goods to other parts. The country from Carmel to Arvad was the mother of colonies, such as Utica, Carthage, and others,[2] and the mistress of the seas, bearing her merchandise far and near (cf. Is 23^{8}, Ezk 26, 27). It was to the interests of Israel to be closely connected with such an enterprising people. Owing to the growth of cities under Ahab, and the increase of the power and splendour of the royal court at Samaria and Jezreel, there must have been a corresponding increase in Israelite commercial activity, though the Biblical records make no reference to it. Much of this, no doubt, found an outlet north-eastward along the great caravan route to Nineveh, *via* Damascus, Riblah, Emesa, Ḥamath, Aleppo,

[1] Contenau, *La Civilization phénicienne* (1926), pp. 299 ff.

[2] Carthage (Phœnician name, Qart Hadasht, 'the new town') was founded on the site of an earlier trading station (Cambē or Caccabē) about 822 B.C. by Elissa (Dido), a great-granddaughter of Ithobaal, who had been dethroned in favour of her brother Pygmalion. Utica, in North Africa, was the most ancient Phœnician colony, founded about 1100 B.C.

Carchemish, and Ḥarran. Ahab, for instance, obtained from the King of Damascus the right to have streets (חֻצוֹת) in that town, *i.e.* an Israelite trading quarter or 'concession' (1 K 20^{34}). But few outlets could equal that of Phœnicia, whose wares were prominent in the markets of the world, and there can be little doubt that much of the commerce of Israel was in the hands of the Phœnicians. Exports also implied imports, so that the Israelites in return for what they could produce easily were able to receive from abroad what they could only produce with difficulty or not at all. The idea that they were cut off, as it were, from the rest of the world, isolated and living apart from other nations, is incorrect. Their manner of life was probably exclusive,[1] but their intercourse and commercial dealings with Egyptians, Phœnicians, Babylonians, Arabs, and other outside peoples were of an intimate kind.[2] There was little difficulty in transport. For this, a light two-wheeled cart or chariot was generally utilized, such as we find represented on the Assyrian bas-reliefs of the period, or engraved on the Carthaginian steles (cf. Nu $7^{3.7.8}$, 1 S 6^{7-10}, 2 S 6^{3}, Am 2^{13}). This was drawn by asses or oxen, while the horse remained, as in Mesopotamia, a more noble animal, reserved for cavalry and war-chariots. Sometimes the chariot was dispensed with, and asses laden with a pack-saddle (with two baskets)

[1] Cf. Josephus, *Cont. Apion*, i. 12.

[2] Cf. Bertholet, *History of Hebrew Civilization*, Eng. ed., p. 28.

were used, not unlike what is found in Syria at the present day. Earthenware representations of these have been unearthed in Phœnicia.[1]

One must not forget, of course, that all this commercial activity of Israel had its dangers, for where the exports emptied the land and left no reserves, trouble and suffering followed. If the harvest failed for want of rain (cf. Am $4^{7ff.}$), or locusts and other larvæ destroyed the fields, vineyards, fig trees, and olive trees (Am 4^{9}), famine raged in the land, otherwise rich and fertile. A man could be bought for a pair of sandals (Am 2^{6}), and then sold to the dealers of Tyre, who provided slaves for the whole world.[2] Amos pours severe reproaches on Tyre for having broken the treaty of friendship between the two countries by delivering large numbers of Jewish slaves to the Edomites (Am 1^{9}). The commerce of Israel, therefore, when conducted without forethought or morality, had its drawbacks. In the hands of unscrupulous men, it tended to develop evils of a peculiar and alarming character. Amos, calling to the Assyrians and Egyptians, says :

> Assemble yourselves upon the mountain[3] of Samaria,
> And behold what great tumults are therein.
> For they know not to do right, saith Yahweh,
> Who store up treasure by violence and robbery.[4]

The commercial fever even led to a disregard of the

[1] Cf. Contenau, *La Civilization phénicienne*, p. 286.

[2] Cf. Renan, *Hist. du peuple d'Israël*, ii. p. 427 ; *Odyssey*, xiv. 288–297 ; Herodotus, i. 1, 2 ; Bérard, *Les Phéniciens et l'Odyssée* (Colin, 1902), i. p. 161 and ii. p. 453 ; cf. also Jl 3^{6} and Ezk 27^{13}.

[3] In the singular, according to LXX.

[4] Am $3^{9,10}$.

usual religious feasts on the ground that they interrupted business :

> When will the new moon be gone, said they,
> That we may sell corn again ?
> And the Sabbath, that we may re-open our stores of wheat ?[1]

These evils probably arose from the commercial development of Israel being too rapid for the economic condition of the land. They do not detract, however, from the policy of Ahab in establishing friendly relations with Phœnicia, and thus securing, among other benefits, trading privileges for his subjects. Commerce everywhere has its evils, such as unfair dealing and greed of gain, but in itself it is not responsible for these, and when properly conducted carries with it many undoubted advantages. The alliance with Phœnicia, from a commercial and political point of view at least, was a wise one.

Egypt at this time does not appear to have played any controlling part in Syrian or Israelite affairs. We read in the Old Testament of an invasion of Judah by Zerah, the 'Ethiopian,' about 895 B.C., and his defeat by Asa. 'Zerah' seems to be a corruption of '(O)zerakh(on),' and may thus represent Osorkon I. of Egypt, who reigned *c.* 925–894 B.C. After this date, however, Egypt appears to have made no further attack on the Palestinian kingdoms, but sank into apathy and indifference. A thousand men of 'Muṣri' (along with the

[1] Am 8^5.

armies of Ahab, Irkhulêni of Ḥamath, Adad-idri of Damascus, and other Syrian kings) are mentioned by Shalmaneser III. as having fought against him at Ḳarḳar, in the Orontes valley, in 853 B.C. Some scholars regard 'Muṣri' here as Egypt, and believe that Osorkon II. (*c.* 874–856 B.C.), stirred by tales of Assyria's ferocious conquests and by fear of possible consequences to his own land, sent this contingent to the aid of Syria, and in support of this view it is said that 'excavations at Samaria have revealed traces of relations between Osorkon and Ahab.'[1] But the presence in the Israelite debris of a fragment of a vase inscribed with Osorkon's name is no proof of such relations. The vase may have reached Samaria in the ordinary way through some Phœnician merchant. The Babylonian and Assyrian term 'Muṣri,' as Schrader pointed out long ago,[2] is known to have applied not only to Egypt but also to a country in the north of Syria adjoining the Taurus Mountains, on the fringe of the old Hittite empire.[3] Thus, Ashur-uballit I. (*c.* 1386–1369 B.C.) is stated to have subdued Muṣri and Shubarî (the latter on the higher Tigris)[4]; Shalmaneser I. (*c.* 1276–1257 B.C.), on his monument found at Ashur, tells us

[1] Dr. Hall, *Cambridge Ancient History*, iii. p. 262.

[2] *Zeitschrift für Assyriologie*, 1874, p. 53.

[3] See Map, *Cambridge Ancient History*, ii. p. 250. The term, especially as applied to Egypt, varies: *Muṣri, Muṣur, Muṣuru.* In the Babylonian versions of the inscriptions of Darius it is *Miṣir*, while in the Amarna Letters it is *Miṣri, Miṣrī, Miṣrîm, Maṣrī*, etc. It is generally derived (very doubtfully) from מָצוֹר, 'fort.'

[4] *Cambridge Ancient History*, ii. p. 234.

that he brought all Muṣri into subjection and continued his victorious campaign by invading Hani, *i.e.* Hanigalbat, north-east of Muṣri [1]; Tiglath-pileser I. (*c.* 1115–1103 B.C.), pushing north-west by Carchemish, fought against revolt in Muṣri, with its city Arina and its district of Ḳumani (*i.e.* Comana) [2]; Shalmaneser III. (*c.* 859–824 B.C.), on his Black Obelisk,[3] describes the tribute he had received from the land of Muṣri: 'Camels with double humps, oxen from the river Sakīya, a *sūsu* (kind of antelope), female elephants, and apes.' [4] In all these cases, judging from the context, the term 'Muṣri' clearly applies not to Egypt but to the northern district to which we have referred. In the case of the battle of Ḳarḳar, we have only to remember that in the list of allied states taking part against Shalmaneser, the order is as follows: Damascus, Ḥamath, Israel, Ḳue, Muṣri, Irḳanata, Arvad, Usanati, Shiana, Syrian desert, the Amanus (or Ammon ?). Muṣri is thus interposed between Ḳue and Irḳanata. If Ḳue was just east of the Cilician Gates, as Assyriologists believe, and if Irḳanata be Irḳata (= Arḳā, Gn 10^{17}) on the Phœnician coast a little south of Arvad, the likelihood is that in this list Muṣri was meant to represent the northern one, which lay

[1] *Cambridge Ancient History*, ii. p. 240.

[2] *Ibid.* p. 248.

[3] See footnote, p. 127.

[4] Hommel, *Hastings' Dictionary*, i. p. 184*a*. Tiglath-pileser I., Ashur-naṣir-pal II., Thutmose I., and Thutmose III. all state that they had hunted elephants in the Mesopotamian regions (cf. Olmstead, *Hist. of Assyr.*, pp. 35, 64).

just north-east of Ḳue.[1] It would seem strange if the scribe had listed the land of the Pharaohs among several north Syrian districts, and between a Cilician and a Phœnician one. Egypt, in fact, seems to have had no share in Palestinian rule at this time. She was perishing through inanition and internal dissension at home. In Syria at least her prestige had long since gone (witness the story of Unamūn, *c.* 1100 B.C.), and it is questionable if she had any garrisons beyond her own confines. So far therefore as Ahab and his kingdom were concerned, she seems to have been outside the sphere of practical politics, except perhaps as a country to deal with commercially through Phœnicia.

The period, in fact, was characterized by a new distribution of political power. The Bubastite dynasty was declining, the Hittite empire had collapsed before successive western hordes, and Assyria with its increasing military power and ever-

[1] The same is probably true of Miṣraim in 1 K $10^{28f.}$, 2 Ch $1^{16f.}$. It is translated Egypt, but according to the amended reading (cf. Peet, *Egypt and the Old Testament*, pp. 155 ff.) Solomon's horses came from Muṣri and Ḳue. It is unlikely, in spite of Dt 17^{16}, that the Egyptians, who had no extensive pastures, could have had an export trade in horses. On the other hand, they imported powerful stallions from north Syria (cf. Maspéro, *The Struggle of the Nations*, p. 215, with references). We know too from Herodotus that these regions were famed for their horse-breeding, and from Ezk (27^{14}) that the Tyrians obtained their horses from Togarmah (*i.e.* either *Tegarama* of the Boghaz-Keui texts, a region lying between Carchemish and Kharput, or *Tilgarimmu* of the Assyrian texts, modern *Gorün*), a place that must have lain within or adjoined the northern Muṣri (cf. Map 1, *Cambridge Ancient History*, iii. p. 1; E. Forrer, *Die Provinzeinteilung des Assyrischen Reiches* (Leipzig, 1921), pp. 75, 84, etc.).

expanding grip was beginning to occupy the stage of history.

This rise of Assyria, bent on reaching the Mediterranean, was the chief factor leading to Ahab's foreign policy, and when properly regarded explains the Aramæan-Israelite wars in his time, which some critics find it difficult to account for. Already, about 1100 B.C., Tiglath-pileser I., King of Assyria, had advanced to the shores of the Mediterranean and taken possession of Arvad as an outlet on the sea, though the Assyrian occupation had only been temporary. About two centuries later, Assyria began to stir as a new organized military power. At first her imperial designs appeared only as a little cloud on the eastern horizon, but soon this began to darken the sky. About the year 875 B.C., the date of Ahab's accession, while the Bubastites were still slumbering, she burst upon the Orontes valley and the Phœnician coast under the conquering leadership of Ashur-naṣir-pal II. There were important reasons besides mere ambition for her advance in this direction. She could not exist commercially without maritime outlets. A large part of her population depended for support upon the traffic in metals, cloth stuffs, and other essential products, which were exported by caravan beyond the Khābūr regions, and it was mainly through the ports of Phœnicia that the traffic found its way westward. Assyria was shut off from any control of it, while Phœnicia, through holding the monopoly, was becoming wealthy and powerful.[1] As a treeless land, Assyria also needed a constant supply of hard timber, which was best obtained from the forests of Lebanon. A bas-relief in the Louvre, taken from the Assyrian palace at Dur-Sharrukin (modern *Khorsabâd*), represents a flotilla of vessels laden with beams being shipped from the Phœnician coast to north Syria, whence they were transported by carriers to Assyria.[2] All the finest kinds of wood—cedars, oaks, walnut trees, pines, cypress trees, and others—existed in the Lebanon in ancient times in great abundance, spreading their perfume for many miles around. The author of the Papyrus Anastasi I., which dates from about the thirteenth century B.C., describes the impenetrable forests there.[3] At this period of expansion, therefore, the Assyrian monarchs made the western lands

[1] Cf. Welch, *The People and the Book*, p. 137.

[2] Cf. Contenau, *La Civilization phénicienne*, p. 282: 'Les bois sont coupés dans le Liban, descendus à la côte, transportés par eau sur un point plus au nord, plus près des routes menant vers l'Assyrie. Là les bois sont déchargés et vont prendre la voie de terre en franchissant les cols de la montagne.'

For a copy of the bas-relief, see E. Pottier, *Catalogue des antiquités assyriennes*, pl. xx.; and for a similar one see Botta and Flandin, *Monuments de Ninive*, i. 33.

[3] To-day this is all changed. In the Lebanon district there remains only one small wood of cedars in the region of *Jebel-el-Khodhid*, near the source of the river *Ḳadisha* (cf. Contenau, *La Civilization phénicienne*, p. 34). Farther south there are no woods west of Jordan except at Nazareth and in the Carmel region. Timber in Palestine is so scarce that it has to be imported, mainly from the southern Alps. Efforts are now being made to rectify this lack. In February 1928 the first saplings of a huge forest (the 'Balfour Forest') of 50,000 trees were planted on a site below Nazareth by Lord Plumer and Sir Alfred Mond.

their objective. Ashur-naṣir-pal invaded Syria and Phœnicia with an immense army, marching along the Lebanon and reaching the coast. He washed his weapons, he tells us, in the Great Sea. 'I received tribute from the kings of the coast, from the people of Tyre, Sidon, Byblus, and Arvad. I received silver, gold, lead, and bronze, thirty-five bronze vases, garments made of brilliantly coloured cloth, ivory, and a dolphin from the sea.'[1] His son and successor, Shalmaneser III. (*c.* 859–824 B.C.),[2] devoted the first three years of his reign to the further conquest of the west, especially of Bit-Adini, a strong sovereign state about 50 miles east of Aleppo, which blocked his march to the Mediterranean. He completely subjugated this kingdom, colonizing and resettling it with Assyrians. Before 856 B.C., the probable date of the siege of Samaria by Adad-idri[3]

[1] Budge and King, *Annals of the Kings of Assyria* (1902), i. pp. 199 f.

[2] Schnabel, by a slight correction of Forrer's arrangement of the eponyms, would make the first eponym year of Shalmaneser III. 857, and would reduce all dependent dates accordingly. But Schnabel's view, though possible, cannot be accepted as certainly correct.

[3] Adad-idri in Assyrian is (*ilu*) IM-idri, where the ideogram IM (𒅎) is read as Rammānu (Rimmon), *i.e.* Adad or Hadad (' the god of storm and thunder'). Hence we have Adad-idri ('Adad is my glory'). How the name came to be translated Ben-Hadad in Scripture is uncertain, but as Adad's name was sometimes written with the ideogram U (𒌋), which could be read as Bur (cf. Prince, *Sumerian Lexicon*, p. 339, l. 3; p. 63, l. 24), it has been assumed that the Hebrew scribes confused this with the Aramaic *bar* ('son'), and translated it into Hebrew as Ben, while *dr* of 'idri' was miswritten *dd*. It is far more likely that the name Ben-Hadad ('son of Hadad') was a general Hebrew one for the kings of Damascus, as in Jer 49^{27}, Am 1^{4} (cf. also 1 K $15^{18ff.}$, 2 K 6 ff. 13^{3}).

of Damascus (1 K 20), Upper Syria had been ravaged, loads of timber had been taken from Mount Amanus, and the cities on the Orontes seized. The desperate resistance of the Aramæan inland states proved of no avail. Tyre, Sidon, and the Phœnician coast towns, which seem to have been largely pro-Assyrian, were still contentedly paying tribute, but several of the Aramæan and Hittite states, under the leadership of Adad-idri, formed themselves into a powerful league of defence to face the increasing menace. The league was mostly composed of states in the north, such as Damascus, Ḥamath, and Arvad, and even included such districts as Ḳue and Muṣri beyond the Amanus.

What was Ahab to do? The siege of Samaria by Adad-idri (Ben-Hadad II.) about 856 B.C., just when the Assyrian monarch was threatening the western states and when the league must have been in process of formation, and the renewed attack at Aphek (? *el-Mejdel*, 15 miles north-west of Samaria) next year, are best explained by the theory that the King of Israel preferred to stay out of such a confederacy, and that some force was being used to bring him into it. He was in close alliance by marriage and otherwise with Phœnicia, whose merchants regarded the Assyrian advance not in the light of conquest but as an opportunity of securing valuable commercial concessions and of linking themselves with what they rightly foresaw was the coming empire of the Near East.[1] As already

[1] Cf. Olmstead, *History of Assyria*, p. 95.

mentioned, there was an extensive commerce between the Mesopotamian regions and Phœnicia. Assyria and Babylonia not only sent their goods westward, but received merchandise from the farther east, and transmitted it onward. The merchants of Tyre, Sidon, and other Phœnician ports were the intermediaries of a great sea traffic between east and west. We need not wonder that all Phœnicia hastened to send gifts to Ashur-naṣir-pal: it is evidence that her towns were prepared to pay any reasonable price, so long as Assyria controlled the trade routes and kept these free from interference. We find that shortly before the date of the siege of Samaria 'the kings of the coast' brought tribute to Shalmaneser. At his camp on the seashore, the two representatives of Tyre and Sidon, accompanied by their sons, advanced in adoration, and behind them came tribute-bearers.[1] For commercial and political reasons, then, neither Tyre nor Sidon nor Byblus entered Adad-idri's league, and these towns were not represented at the great battle of Ḳarḳar (*c.* 853 B.C.) that followed. Only places in the extreme north of Phœnicia, such as Irḳanata and Arvad, which were largely of Hittite extraction and sympathy, thought it expedient to join. This pro-Assyrian attitude of certain states explains why Ashur-naṣir-pal was able to march unopposed to the Mediterranean. 'It is difficult to under-

[1] For the figure representing the incident, see *Revue archéologique*, iv. 23.

stand,' says Sidney Smith, 'why Ashur-naṣir-pal was able without a blow to imitate so exactly the exploits of Tiglath-pileser in the west, unless there was an Assyrian party working in his favour. . . . It is not fanciful then to compare Ashur-naṣir-pal's relations with Syria to those of Philip of Macedon with Greece.' [1]

It is probable therefore that Ahab, owing to his ties with Phœnicia, could not be persuaded to join the league without some compulsion from Adad-idri and his allies. He may, in fact, have had some pro-Assyrian sympathies. It has been conjectured that his father, Omri, paid tribute to Assyria, and even owed his throne to Assyrian help. The kingdom of Israel would be relieved too by the advance of Assyria from the Aramæan domination of Damascus, just as later Jeroboam was probably relieved by the Assyrian campaigns and thus enabled to 'restore the boundary of Israel' (2 K 14^{25}). Both under Baasha and Omri districts of Israelite territory had been annexed to the state of Damascus, and Ahab no doubt felt that the way to political salvation and national prosperity did not lie in coalition with such a state, but rather in alliance, or at least agreement, with Assyria, whose powerful military assistance was worth having when needed.

Hence Adad-idri and the other parties to the league found it necessary to show their strength to Ahab and bring pressure to bear on him. They

[1] *Cambridge Ancient History*, iii. p. 15.

realized that this was better than losing the help of his well-organized army and numerous chariots and leaving a neutral or pro-Assyrian state in their rear. This accounts for the siege of Samaria and the large number of confederate kings who joined in the attack (1 K 20[1]). We have cases of an identical kind in the history of the period. Thus, from a stele found at Afis in north Syria in 1903, we learn that Zakir (or Zakar), King of Ḥamath and Luʿash, was besieged in Hazrak (Hadrach, Zec 9[1]) by 'Bar-Hadad, son of Hazael, King of Aram,' and a confederation of seventeen Aramæan kings, including those of Ḳue, ʿAmk (Cœle-Syria, or perhaps Antioch), Gurgum (adjoining Muṣri), Sam'āl (modern *Zenjirli*, at the Amanus Mountains), and others. 'All these kings laid siege against Hazrak, and raised a wall higher than the wall of Hazrak, and made a trench deeper than its trench. And I lifted up my hands to the Baal-Shamēn, and he answered me, and spoke to me by the hand of seers and calculators (?). . . . Fear not, for I have made [thee k]ing, [and I will st]and by thee, and I will deliver thee from all [these ki]ngs who have made [siege-works against thee] . . ." [1] It seems that this king, who was evidently Semitic, judging by his name (cf. Zaccur,

[1] S. A. Cook, *Cambridge Ancient History*, iii. p. 376. For the inscription, see H. Pognon, *Inscr. sémit. de la Syrie* (1907), pp. 156 ff.; Lidzbarski, *Ephem.* (1909), iii. pp. 1–11; Driver, *Expositor*, June 1908, p. 481; J. Barth and H. Grimme, *Orientalistische Litteraturzeitung*, 1909, cols. 10 and 13; Torrey, *Journal of the American Orient. Soc.*, xxxv. (1917), pp. 353 ff.

Zachariah), was supporting the Assyrian cause at the time of Adad-nirari's campaign in the west (*c.* 805–802 B.C.), and consequently found himself in the same position as Ahab half a century earlier. We know, too, how Ahaz of Judah, who was friendly with Assyria and would not enter the defensive league formed by Rezon of Damascus and Pekah of Samaria, was besieged in Jerusalem by the Syro-Ephraimite army, and a large number of captives was carried off (2 Ch 28; cf. Is 7). Cases like these seem to show that Ahab may have had pro-Assyrian sympathies, and that the Israelites, like the Phœnicians, were profiting from the patronage of Assyria. Some scholars, such as Dr. S. A. Cook, who have found difficulty in correlating the Assyrian and Biblical accounts, would transpose the whole Aramæan-Israelite conflict to the time of the Jehu dynasty. But there is no need for this. The fact that certain wars or incidents 'naturally illustrate' a succeeding dynasty or are 'in marked agreement' with it is no reason why they should be transferred to it, especially when their present situation is in perfect accord with the conditions; and though some of the stories of siege and battle are anonymous (1 K 20$^{23-34}$, and note v.^{34}), as Dr. Cook reminds us, this does not necessarily imply that they have been wrongly placed by the editors. The theory of Wellhausen[1] that Adad-idri's attacks on Samaria took place *after* the battle of Ḳarḳar is founded on a

[1] Article 'Israel' in *Ency. Brit.*

similar misunderstanding of the international position, for it involves the view that Ahab was a powerful supporter of the anti-Assyrian league up to that time (*c.* 853 B.C.), while it is also in serious disagreement with the chronology, for it throws Ahab's death several years later, and thus leaves only five or six years for the combined reigns of Ahaziah and Jehoram.

The result of the attack on Ahab must have been more successful than the Biblical record admits. It should be remembered that the Israelitish traditions in the Book of Kings are derived from two very different sources: one dealing mainly with the work of the prophets (*e.g.* 1 K 17–19, 21), and the other with the royal annals (*e.g.* 1 K 20, 22). The latter is naturally coloured by patriotic feelings and shows a strong partiality for the warrior king. It is highly probable, as Van Doorminck and Wellhausen have pointed out,[1] that the narrative of the siege of Samaria and of the battle of Aphek (1 K 20) which followed has received many interpolations at the hands of well-meaning scribes which tend to make the deliverance of the Israelites greater than it was. Possibly the result of the struggle was somewhat indecisive, but the power of Adad-idri and his huge confederacy of Hittite and Aramæan kings was sufficient to force Ahab into friendly agreement. It is pretty certain that the advantages of joining

[1] Doorminck, *Theologisch Tijdschrift*, 1895, pp. 576–584; Wellhausen, *Die Composition des Hexateuchs*, pp. 285 f.

the alliance formed a subject of conversation between the two kings, and that Ahab was glad to get rid of a crushing and exhausting war by promising the help of his forces. This theory of the result is not rendered improbable, as some think, by the fact that he was able to furnish such a large contingent (see below) to the army which met Shalmaneser, for the numbers on the Assyrian inscription are probably exaggerated, as some of the town-states mentioned could not have mustered the forces attributed to them. Besides, the Hittite-Aramæan combined armies (those of 'thirty-two kings') which attacked him must have been much more formidable and imposing than his own army. Nor is the theory affected by the story (1 K 20^{35-42}) condemning him for his leniency and foretelling his destruction, for this is believed to be a later popular one, akin in tone to 1 K 13. In return for Ahab's assistance, the covenant (בְּרִית) entered into promised the return of the Israelite cities taken from Omri, and conceded special quarters ('streets') in Damascus for Israelite merchants. This satisfactory *quid pro quo* probably helped Ahab to decide as he did.

At the battle of Ḳarḳar (? Apamea, modern *Ḳala'at el-Mudîḳ*, on the Orontes, north of Ḥamath) that followed, Shalmaneser was now confronted with the most considerable force that the rising power of Assyria had ever met: in round numbers about 63,000 infantry, 2000 light cavalry, 4000 chariots, and 1000 camels. Their composition, which occurs only on his Monolith (col. ii. ll. 90–95), is:

	CHARIOTS.	CAVALRY.	INFANTRY.
Adad-idri of Damascus .	1200	1200	20,000
Irkhulêni of Ḥamath .	700	700	10,000
Aẖabbu Sir-'i-lai . .	2000	..	10,000
Ḳue	..	..	500
Muṣri	..	..	1,000
Irḳanata	10	..	10,000
Matinu-ba'ali of Arvad .	..	..	200
Usanati	..	..	200
Adunu-ba'li of Shiana .	30	..	10,000
Gindibu', the Arab .	..	1000 (camels)	..
Ba'sa, son of Rukhubi, of the Amanus (or of Ammon?) . . .	..	..	1,000

As this list on the Monolith [1] contains no mention of Judah, some critics hold the view that the southern kingdom was in vassalage to Israel at this time, and that its troops are included among Ahab's, but the obvious reason for its non-mention seems rather to be that it lay entirely outside the political field and was not in the confederacy, which was limited to the north. Shalmaneser claims as a matter of

[1] Shalmaneser's annals are chiefly to be found engraved on three monuments now in the British Museum, namely: the Monolith, containing a full-length figure of him, with an inscription (for this, see Schrader, *Cuneiform Inscriptions and the O.T.*, i. 183 f.); the Black Obelisk (marble), found at Calah by Sir A. H. Layard, which has twenty small bas-reliefs on the upper portions of its four sides representing tribute-bearers, as well as accompanying inscriptions; and the Bronze Bands found in 1878 at *Balâwât*, which belong to four gates and contain scenes in *repoussé* work with short texts of explanation added. The Obelisk and Bands are two of the finest Assyrian works of art extant.

course to have been victorious, but as his records vary by more than a hundred per cent. in the number of the enemies killed, his claim may be regarded as doubtful.[1] That his own losses were heavy is shown by the fact that he abandoned the campaign and withdrew northward again without even assaulting Ḳarḳar or advancing on Ḥamath. The league continued in existence, but Ahab at least took advantage of Adad-idri's losses (which must have been large) and the blow dealt to that leader's power to shake himself free; and towards the end of the same year (853 B.C.), or perhaps early the next year ('the time when kings go forth to battle' (2 S 11[1]) was the spring-time), having secured the assistance of Jehoshaphat of Judah, he endeavoured to wrest Ramoth-Gilead from Damascus, but was defeated, severely wounded, and died in his chariot on the battlefield. Some who cannot understand Ahab thus attacking Damascus after being a member of the league would place his death *before* the battle

[1] The Monolith gives the number killed as 14,000, the Obelisk as 20,500, Bull No. 1 as 25,000, and an inscription found at Ashur as 29,000. It is clear that the main interest of the Assyrian annalists, like the Egyptian ones, was the glorification of their monarchs, and too much reliance must not be placed on figures quoted. As another case of the same kind, the *Balâwât* inscription gives the number of enemies killed on a certain occasion by Shalmaneser as 300, while the Monolith makes it 3400. The value of the various Assyrian sources must be determined on the principle that in general the most faithful and complete account is the first, the one nearest to the date of the events. In the process of years, the number of towns taken or enemies killed or captured grew inordinately. Cf. Jean, *La Littérature des Babyloniens et des Assyriens*, 1924, pp. 236 f.; Thureau-Dangin, *Une Relation de la huitième campagne de Sargon*, 1912, pp. xix and xx.

of Ḳarḳar,[1] and suggest that his name on the Monolith has been confused with that of his successor, Jehoram. But apart from the fact that this procedure involves a rejection or modification of archæological evidence in order to support a chronological theory, such a view overlooks Ahab's probable disinclination to enter the league, and his natural desire to clear out of it at the earliest opportunity.

It was not till 849 B.C., four years after Ahab's death, that Shalmaneser returned to the charge, battling against Adad-idri and his confederacy on the Orontes in much the same locality as before, but with the same indecisive result. Three years later, he made another attempt against them, but effected no more. In 841, however, after Adad-idri's death, and the consequent break-up of the league, he launched a fourth campaign which virtually sealed the fate of the Aramæan states. He defeated Hazael, the new king of Damascus, a military usurper, at Mount Saniru (Hermon, Dt 3^9, cf. Ca 4^8) in the northern part of Anti-Lebanon, inflicting on him the loss of 16,000 men, and thus opening the road to the Mediterranean. Crossing Phœnicia unopposed, he reached the coast at *Nahr el-Kelb* (north of *Beirût*), where he cut his relief in the rocks and received tribute from Tyre and Sidon. Jehu of Israel, who like the Phœnicians had stood out of the Damascus league, was among the tribute-bearers.

[1] Cf. Horner, *Proc. Soc. Bibl. Arch.*, 1898, p. 244; Kamphausen, *Chron. of Heb. Kings*, p. 80.

On the Black Obelisk (the second panel from the top) his ambassadors, men in long-fringed robes with short sleeves and caps like turbans, are depicted as presenting gold and silver bars, a golden vase and a golden spoon, cups and goblets of gold, pieces of lead (or tin), a staff for the king's hand, and some spear-shafts. He is referred to in the inscription as '*Ia-ua, son of Ḫumrî*.'[1] For both Israel and Judah, as well as the neighbouring states, this victorious march of Shalmaneser's was the beginning of the end. Gradually Assyria managed to break down every barrier, and obtained a strangle-hold on all Palestine.

The repeated Assyrian campaigns, the formation and breaking-up of the Aramæan-Hittite league, and the great dynastic changes resulting must have involved profound internal political activities in Israel, and especially in the city of Samaria. Unfortunately, neither the campaigns nor the league nor the political vicissitudes are mentioned by the Biblical historian. Ahab is judged from the prophetico-didactic point of view which held the field two or three centuries later under totally different national conditions. His statesmanship, political far-sightedness, and military splendour are passed over without reference. His prominence in the record arises only from the fact that he came

[1] Shalmaneser's inscription, detailing his victory and the tribute received, will be found in Rawlinson, *Cuneiform Inscriptions of Western Asia*, iii. 5, No. 6; Jean, *La Littér. des Babyl. et Assyr.*, 1924, pp. 250 f.; King, *First Steps in Assyrian*, pp. 37 ff.

into collision with the prophetic order, and as a rule only those national events in his life are detailed which were interwoven with the grand and sombre traditions of Elijah. For 'the rest of his acts, his wars, and all that he did' we are relegated to the sources which the writer himself used. What would we not give for a Biblical account of the relations between Israel and Assyria, or the pressing circumstances leading to the league, or Israel's part in the battle of Ḳarḳar? On all these and other national matters of importance, we cannot but regret the meagreness of the records.

CHAPTER VII

THE RELIGIOUS SITUATION

THERE is considerable difficulty in determining the exact religious situation in Israel in the ninth century, especially during the reign of Ahab. The varied material we have in 1 Kings is fragmentary and uncertain, consisting of only a few of the outstanding traditions that must have prevailed. The age was crowded with religious activity, yet so few particulars have survived that one can hardly form a complete and trustworthy picture. It is not until a century later, during the lifetime of the first literary prophets Amos and Hosea, that we have independent evidence to help us. Moreover, the history in its present form is by no means contemporary: the old traditions, some of which undoubtedly go back to a very early period, have been so re-shaped and modified in the course of time that the task of recovering them, in the absence of external evidence, is far from easy. If we accept the Grafian theory, as most scholars do, as the basis for the reconstruction of Israel's religion and literature, the old traditions came under priestly influence many ages after they had been committed to writing.[1] Samuel-Kings, as it stands, is the result of late compilations and didactic treatment. Its main editing did not take place till the latter days of the Judæan monarchy (*c.* 600 B.C.), and it must have received still later redactional additions and interpolations bringing it down to the release of Jehoiachin (*c.* 561), and in all probability to a period several years later (2 K 25^{30}). Its final religious standpoint is thus based upon the Book of the Law (probably the main parts of Deuteronomy) discovered in 621 B.C. The compilers and editors are deeply influenced by the spirit of this book, and their language partakes largely of its characteristic phraseology. They view the past, including the actions and characters of the early kings, in the light of the circumstances and events of their own late age, and even reflect their own beliefs in the speeches and prophecies recorded. Their aim is didactic, having a definite religious purpose—to exhibit the course of history as so controlled by Jahweh, that faithfulness to Him ensured blessing and unfaithfulness to Him led to His displeasure and to consequent national decline (cf. 2 K $17^{7-23.\ 32.\ 41}$ $23^{26f.}$). The standpoint, too, as we have said (p. 108), is entirely Judæan, influenced by an antipathy to Samaria. The northern kingdom is regarded unfavourably, as having been founded

[1] According to the Grafian theory, put forward by K. H. Graf, a pupil of Reuss, towards the end of 1865, and upheld by Kuenen, Duhm, Wellhausen, Stade, and other critics, the priestly writings are the latest, coming after the Pentateuchal documents and even after Ezekiel.

on the calf-cult of Jeroboam I., and as unclean, wicked, and apostate. The close interrelations that existed in Ahab's time and probably at other periods are forgotten or overlooked. The result of all this editing and modifying is to create some uncertainty as to what were the original authentic traditions.[1] It also leaves us without accurate chronological data, as well as with discrepancies and contradictions difficult to harmonize (cf. 2 K 8^{25} with 9^{29}; 2 K 15^{30} with 15^{33}). It is evident that, to obtain a proper view of the religious situation in Ahab's time, allowances must be made for these characteristics of the Biblical record. It is only by a careful study of the problem, assisted by external and contemporary evidence, that one can hope to arrive at a just estimate.

The central figures in the religious history are Elijah and Elisha. The attention of the writers, in fact, is so largely occupied with the activity of these prophets that little room is left for other matters.

[1] The original narratives themselves, especially in the case of the religious situation in Ahab's time, must be dated not long after the activity of Elijah and Elisha. Even advanced critics admit that only a few decades lie between these men and the original record of their activity. Cf. Duhm, *Israels Propheten*, p. 84; Steuernagel, *Einleitung in das Alte Testament*, p. 370; Sellin, *Der alttestamentliche Prophetismus*, p. 18; *Introduction to the Old Testament*, p. 124; Gunkel, *Elias, Jahve, und Baal*, p. 44. As Dr. Peake states (*Elijah and Jezebel*, p. 24), 'The narratives do not reflect the ideas of the great eighth-century prophets. There is no attack on the worship of the calves, no insistence on the necessity for the centralization of worship at a single sanctuary, no attack on astral worship.' The difficulty is to disentangle these original narratives from the editorial additions and modifications of later ages.

Some critics would say that the prophetic aspect has been overcoloured or drawn too prominently, and that the parallelism between the Elijah cycle of stories and the Elisha one is, to say the least, suspicious. But the matter cannot be dismissed in this way. The stern Elijah steps abruptly on the stage as an extraordinary personality. His sudden appearances and disappearances are remarkable. We have a picture of the country suffering from a terrible drought of more than two years' duration, due to the Divine displeasure at Jezebel's persecution of the prophets for opposing the cult of the Tyrian Baal; but at last, after Elijah as the champion of Yahweh has defeated the priests of Baal at an imposing scene on Mount Carmel, the drought ceases.[1] At the scene referred to, while the prophets of Baal cry and cut themselves with knives and dance wildly around in order to awaken their god, Elijah stands with outstretched hands beside the restored altar of Yahweh and prays in ordered and reasoned speech.[2] We have another picture of

[1] According to Menander of Ephesus, quoted by Josephus (*Antiq.* VIII. xiii. 2), there was a drought at this time in Phœnicia, lasting for one year, and it was removed through the prayers of Ithobaal, the priest-king. When 'he made supplication, there came great thunders.' As Carmel, which was the scene of Yahweh's victory over Baal and of the ending of the drought, belonged at times to Phœnicia, it is probable that we have here a Phœnician version of the same event, perhaps an older tradition.

[2] The idea suggested by Hitzig in his *Geschichte Israels*, and revived in recent times by Saintyves (*Essais de folklore bibliques*, 1922), that Elijah used naphtha to kindle the sacrifice, is discussed by Dr. Peake, *Elijah and Jezebel*, p. 12. 'Even if Elijah could have descended to such a trick,' he says, 'which I do not for a moment believe, how

him, in a kind of magical light, hearing in advance the rushing of the rain, and running before Ahab's chariot from Carmel to Jezreel (at least a five hours' journey), sustained by the hand of Yahweh (*i.e.* in an ecstatic condition produced by Yahweh). We read of him appearing suddenly before Ahab to condemn the king in the very height of his power for having invaded the rights of Naboth, and proclaiming a stern message to him in the name of the outraged Yahweh, who is the ultimate defender of all justice and right. We have a graphic description of a flight for his life to Horeb, 'the mount of God,' where he lodges in 'the cave,' *i.e.* the cleft in the rock where Moses was believed to have stood (Ex 33^{22}). There he witnesses a most impressive theophany and receives a command to return to Israel, where his work would be finished by the cleansing swords of Hazael of Damascus and of Jehu, and by the coming of Elisha. His ministry finds a fitting conclusion in the story of his extraordinary end—his translation to heaven in a fiery chariot with fiery horses. Whether this story belongs to the original Elijah narratives or whether it has not rather displaced an older narrative of his end, is open to dispute. But in any case, it is strong evidence of the profound impression he produced on his countrymen, as a leader whose activity could only be thought of as enduring, and whose fellowship with Yahweh was so close that it

could he have successfully carried it through under the vigilant eyes of the king and so many spectators . . . ?'

could not be interrupted. Interspersed with such narratives are stories or statements showing other marvels connected with Elijah and the prophets, and the large part these men occupied in the political affairs of the kingdom.

All this prophetical emphasis may have been intended, as some critics think, for 'the glorification of the prophets,'[1] but its existence is not to be explained in this way. The prominence of Elijah in the record is so impressive and tremendous that we need some colossal movement to account for it. That he was a genuine historic character cannot be questioned, although his actions have doubtless received some poetic and legendary embellishment in the prophetic schools. Even Hölscher, who regards the traditions about him as almost entirely legendary and the narratives as unhistorical, admits that he must have been an historical figure.[2] Wellhausen, too, though he insists on the legendary nature of the narratives, only finds in this a proof of the prophet's greatness.[3] The fact is that the unique position Elijah occupied in the imagination and hopes of the people can only be accounted for on the ground that he was an outstanding landmark in the history of Israel, the greatest since the era of Mosaism. There are particular resemblances indeed between Moses and him. As the former inaugurated

[1] T. K. Cheyne, *Ency. Bib.*, 'Ahab.'

[2] Hölscher, *Die Profeten*, p. 177; *Geschichte der israelitischen und jüdischen Religion*, p. 95.

[3] Wellhausen, *Israelitische und jüdische Geschichte* (7th ed.), p. 73.

a new epoch in the religious history of the Hebrew race, so now Elijah appears as the leader of a new religious enthusiasm, bent on far-reaching internal changes. He stands out as the most conspicuous personality next to Moses, and must represent some vast conflict embodied in a single individual, some great radical change, some sweeping movement in favour of a purer Yahwism. It is probable that the movement came from the southern desert, brought into the land by Hebrew nomads. Yahwism was particularly associated with the south (Dt 33², Hab 3³). Its birthplace was there among the desert clans in the Sinai-Kadesh region, as Professor Eduard Meyer, Dr. Bernhard Luther, Professor T. K. Cheyne, Professor Luckenbill and others have shown,[1] and it is not likely that Judah was ever so much cut off from that region as to lose its connection with the ancient shrine and the desert God. It is in the J-document, generally recognized as a southern one, that the name Yahweh is dominant. It is noteworthy, too, that it was to Horeb in the south that Elijah fled, and it seems as if through him a revival of Yahwism, or perhaps a new conception of it, was making its way northward and Samaria was now feeling its influence.[2] It is significant that when Jehu made himself king, at Elisha's bidding, and

[1] Meyer, *Die Israeliten und ihre Nachbarstämme*, pp. 84–88; Luckenbill, on 'Israel's Origins,' in *American Journal of Theology*, xxii. (1918), pp. 24–53.

[2] Cf. J. M. Powis Smith, *American Journal of Semitic Languages and Literatures*, xxxv. (1918), p. 13.

rooted out the Baal cult for the time being, his policy of reformation had the approval of Jehonadab the Rechabite, the representative of a puritan guild which had desert connections (cf. 2 K 10^{15}, Jer $35^{6ff.}$) and which upheld the simpler ideals of life and religion. The purification of Yahweh worship and the reconstruction of a decadent civilization in Canaan received a ready welcome from these nomads.[1] 'It is not unlikely,' says Dr. Peake, 'that the Rechabite movement itself took shape at this time, and embodied a protest against the policy of the royal house.'[2] All these considerations that we have mentioned go to show that the prominent position occupied by Elijah in the Biblical record, though it may be overcoloured, is not exaggerated. It is but the echo of some great religious convulsion, connected by tradition with his name, and probably influenced by the desert.

This view of the matter involves the placing of Elijah and the earlier prophets on a higher pedestal than they generally occupy. According to Wellhausen, who attaches too little value to their position and work,[3] the struggle with Baal cannot have possessed the importance attributed to it, and Israel could never have been torn asunder by such a

[1] For the Rechabites, see Peake's *Commentary on Jeremiah*, ii. pp. 144–146; Lucien Gautier, *Études sur la religion d'Israël* (1927), pp. 104 ff.; E. Meyer, *Die Israeliten und ihre Nachbarstämme*, pp. 132 ff., 166 f.; cf. also Peake, *Elijah and Jezebel* (Manchester University Press), p. 7.

[2] Peake, *Elijah and Jezebel*, p. 9.

[3] *Prolegomena*, 290 ff.

religious commotion. Kuenen, Stade, Duhm, and other critics, as well as Wellhausen, are inclined to depreciate the religion of Israel from its foundation by Moses until the coming of the great eighth century prophets. But such a theory as to the development of the religion is too radical. A critical study of the situation as far back as the ninth century gives evidence that the prophets of that time had a very large share in reshaping, the social, religious, and political conditions. Elijah was a mighty personality, standing between two eras—that of the ancient Hebrews and that of the literary prophets. He stood alone, in solitary grandeur, 'before the face of God.' He was a voice from the desert, calling for the purifying of Yahwism from a pernicious Baalism; the upholder of a severe simplicity in worship as against an elaborate cultus dependent on large bodies of priests; the representative of a rigid puritanism as opposed to a religion of sensuality; the proclaimer of an impartial democratic justice (witness the vineyard of Naboth) trodden under foot by those who thirsted for power and wealth; the mouthpiece of Yahwism protesting against anything that sapped the moral basis of the state. His was the call to lift Yahwism out of the pit of superstition and of a gross civilization into the higher altitude of ethical and spiritual reality. He had no standards: he established his own standard, impelled by a voice within. On Carmel, when putting Baal worship to the test, he utterly ignored the priests of Yahweh (who must have been numerous, considering the number of shrines in the land), and himself assumed the function of sacrificing priest.[1] He imitated no one, for there was no outstanding predecessor save Moses to imitate. He was abrupt, brave, unpolished, but he was himself. He could not occupy this position without the sincerity and faith of a spiritual giant; and embodying, as he does, some sweeping movement of an austere desert type, we cannot say that the Biblical record places too much emphasis on him. It puts him just where tradition must have left him. The view which is inclined to deal so much with post-exilic developments leaves too little room for such a great figure and the movement that he inaugurated. The internal history of Israel would be improved if it were re-shaped so as to give a larger place to such a great reformer.[2]

Elijah's effort for a truer type of Yahwism found ready opportunity in Ahab's kingdom, where the cult of Melḳart, the Tyrian Baal, had been introduced through the king's marriage with Jezebel. In Phœnicia, as in Palestine generally, there was not one god Baal worshipped under different forms, but a multitude of local Baals, each the 'lord' of

[1] The case of Samuel who habitually offered sacrifices is not quite parallel, as he was a Kohathite and thus belonged to a Levite family closely related to the Aaronites (1 Ch 6^{33-38}). In abnormal circumstances the Levites seem to have performed priestly functions, as in Hezekiah's Passover (2 Ch 29^{34}).

[2] Cf. S. A. Cook, *Cambridge Ancient History*, iii. p. 416.

his own district and the protector and benefactor of those who worshipped him there. These Baals were designated according to the place to which they belonged. Thus, we find Baal-rosh ('lord of the promontory'), Baal-saphōn ('lord of the north'), Baal-shamim ('lord of the skies'), and Baal-Lebanon ('lord of the Lebanon'), just as we have Zeus-Casios, *i.e.* Jupiter of Mount Cassius (one of the peaks of the Lebanon).[1] Melḳart ('god of the town') was a name applied to the Baal of Tyre, whose temple according to a tradition in Herodotus (ii. 44) was founded as far back as 2740 B.C. He was later identified by the Greeks with Heracles.[2] At first his characteristics were entirely solar, but later, owing to the natural tendency of the coast towns to connect much of their religion with their sea commerce, he came to be regarded largely as a maritime divinity.[3] He was believed to have perished on a burning pile (as Heracles did), and in memory of his death an annual fête was held at Tyre, at which his effigy was solemnly burned.[4] As Ithobaal, the father of Jezebel, was priest of Astarte, the Sidonian Baalath,[5] there is reason to

[1] In a treaty between Esarhaddon (*c.* 681 B.C.) and the King of Tyre, which deals with the transport of Assyrian booty from the south to the north of Phœnicia, the following gods are cited as Phœnician ones: Baal-shamim, Baal-malki, Baal-saphōn, Melḳart, Eshmun, and Astarte. Cf. Winckler, *Altor. Forschungen*, ii. p. 10.

[2] *Corpus Inscript. Semit.*, 122, *c.* 180 B.C.

[3] Contenau, *La Civil. phén.*, p. 109.

[4] Originally, in place of the effigy, human victims were probably sacrificed on a pyre.

[5] Josephus, *Cont. Apion*, i. 18.

believe that the worship of this female divinity, whose prototype was the Assyrian Ishtar, also received some impetus in Israel. In Assyro-Babylonia, she was principally the goddesss of war, but throughout all Western Asia she was the mother deity, representing productivity and fertility, and like Aphrodite the Cyprian goddess of sensual passion, with whom she came to be identified, she was frequently associated with rites of an unchaste character (hence her cult may be referred to in such passages as Hos $4^{13.14}$, Jer 2^{20}, etc.). Though centred in Sidon, where she had a magnificent temple, which Lucian visited (*De Dea Syria*, § 4), she was a prominent divinity among the Phœnicians generally, and was certainly worshipped in early times by the less faithful Israelites (cf. Jg 2^{13} 10^{6}, 1 S $7^{3.4}$ 12^{10}).[1] One can understand how, with the priestly caste of Phœnicia as close allies of Ahab, the spread of these Phœnician cults in Samaria and other Israelite towns was a natural result. Phœnicia and Israel had become 'brother peoples' (cf. Am 1^{9}), with much closer intercourse between them than the Biblical narrative suggests, and the erection of Baal temples and altars in Israel was bound to follow.

From superficial observation one might say that

[1] The name Astarte occurs in the O.T. as *Ashtôreth*, a vocalization which perhaps arose through the Massoretes, in their religious zeal, maliciously substituting the vowels '*o*, *e*,' to signify that whenever the name occurred it was to be replaced by the Hebrew word '*bôsheth*,' 'shame.'

the difference between Baalism in general and the worship of Yahweh was trifling, and that Elijah was inconsistent in taking such stern repressive measures against the former. The word Baal, being a generic appellative (denoting 'master' or 'owner,' probably of the soil), and not a proper name,[1] was often applied by the Israelites to Yahweh Himself (cf. Hos $2^{16. 17}$).[2] To them Yahweh *was* Baal. Such names as Jerubaal (Gideon), Eshbaal (son of Saul), Meribbaal (son of Jonathan and also son of Saul), Baaljada (or Eljada, son of David), Baaliah ('Baal is Jah,' the designation of one of David's men), and others prove that there was no scruple in using the term Baal at this time in regard to the God of Israel,[3] though the practice was afterwards discouraged by the prophets (cf. Hos 2^{17}), and finally disappeared. The two bull images placed by Jeroboam in the border cities of Dan and Bethel (probably with the object of weakening the supremacy of Jerusalem) were called 'Baalim' by their devotees, and yet were worshipped under the idea that they represented Yahweh. They were not intended by Jeroboam to involve an apostasy from the God of Israel (he called his son and destined successor Abijah, 'Yahweh is my father'), nor

[1] Cf. Jg $2^{11. 13}$, etc., where the article is used.

[2] Objection has been taken by Wellhausen, Nowack, and some other scholars to this passage, which they regard as a later addition. Cf. especially Marti, 'Dodekapropheten' (in *Kurzer Hdcom.*, Tübingen, 1903), pp. 27 ff. But their rejection of it is too *a priori*, and if carried out would involve chapter iii. also.

[3] Cf. Moore on Jg 6^{32}, with references there given.

were they felt by the Israelites at that epoch to be an unorthodox introduction. In the Elijah and Elisha narratives there is not a trace of any polemic against their worship: it was only in later ages, and from a Judæan standpoint, that an unfavourable view was taken of the matter.[1]

Both Baal and Yahweh too were worshipped with similar sacrifices and accompaniments. The Phœnician temple, consisting essentially of a sacred enclosure open to the sky, such as existed at Byblus (according to the representation on a coin of the Emperor Macrin, c. 164–218 A.D.), at Baetocece in the Lebanon (modern *Hosn-Sôleiman*), at Arvad, or at Sidon (according to the researches of Macridy Bey), was practically the same as the Israelite ones. The upright stone or pillar (מַצֵּבָה, *maṣṣēbā*),[2] as the symbol of Baal, and the wooden pole (אֲשֵׁרָה, *Ashērā*),[3] representing the ancient sacred tree, differed in no respect from those which were erected in the worship of Yahweh.[4] There is abundant

[1] The 'bull of Jacob' was a term used of Yahweh Himself (Gn 49²⁴, where אַבִּיר ('bull,' cf. Is 10¹³) should be read for אָבִיר ('the mighty one'). Cf. J. Barth, *Nominalbildung*, 51.). In one of the names on the Samaria *ostraka* (No. 41, עגליו, 'Agalyo or 'Egelyo) which is common in Palmyrene records, the calf (עֵגֶל) and Yahweh are apparently equated.

[2] Wrongly translated 'image' in Authorized Version. Cf. Ex 23²⁴, Lv 26¹, 2 K 3², etc.

[3] Wrongly translated 'grove' in Authorized Version. Cf. Jg 6²⁵ᶠᶠ·, 1 K 14²³, 2 K 18⁴, etc.

[4] In both cases also the pillar seems to have been regarded as the shrine of the divinity, who was considered in some sense to reside in it, or be attached to it. The pillars mentioned in the history of Jacob (Gn 31⁴⁵ 35²⁰, cf. Jos 24²⁶) were primarily not so much memorial

evidence, indeed, that in the pre-Deuteronomic period (*i.e.* until the seventh century at least, as generally regarded) [1] the two cults were inextricably blended, and no evil connotation was attached by the Israelites at that period to the local sanctuaries on mountains and hills (*bâmôth*, 'high places'), which are considered by scholars generally to be denounced by the Deuteronomic redactors (cf. 1 S 9^{2-14}, 1 K 3^{3}, with Dt $12^{2.3}$). Neither Amos nor Hosea betrays any consciousness that these local sanctuaries were illegal, and Elijah was grieved because some of the altars had been thrown down.

Moreover, it must not be forgotten that the Israelites borrowed to a large extent from the Canaanites not only their language, their writing, and their civil and political organizations, but also their religious practices. When the Israelites entered Canaan, the worship of Baal was everywhere present, and was still influenced by what had preceded it—animism, polydæmonism, and ancestor-worship, along with such primitive institutions as totemism, magic, and taboo. They found feasts

stones as dwelling-places of Yahweh. It was the stone of Bethel, not the place, that was called a 'house of God' (Gn 28^{22}). Cf. the name of the *maṣṣēbā* of Shechem, 'El, God of Israel' (Gn 33^{20}). In later ages the belief arose that these βαίτυλοι or βαιτύλια were endowed with magic powers.

[1] Professor A. C. Welch would prefer to date the Code of Deuteronomy from the early monarchy or even from the period of the Judges (Welch, *Code of Deuteronomy*, 1924), while other scholars such as Hölscher would bring it down to about 500 B.C., though still retaining the Grafian sequence.

and sacrifices, shrines and poles, dolmens and altars, all waiting for them. They took possession of many of Baal's high places and substituted the worship of Yahweh. Mohammed did the same with the heathen shrine at Mecca: he destroyed its idols and bound it to sacred memories. The Roman Church, too, adopted feasts of pagan origin, infusing into them a new meaning. This assimilation, however, had its perils to Israel, for the rites and religious festivals of the old Baal cult, especially those connected with the various agricultural seasons, became largely those of Yahwism. After all, the Israelites had received no ritual tradition from Moses, and were not disobeying any injunction of his, but the result was that a Baalized worship of Yahweh developed (cf. Jg 2^{11-13}). The sensual nature-worship and other evil tendencies which had characterized the older cult continued to manifest themselves beneath the new external symbols.

The numerous images, too, unearthed in Palestine, of Astartes or 'mother-goddesses,' representing a girl of licentious pleasures, together with the occurrence of such place-names as 'Ashtārôth (the 'Astartes'), and 'Anāthôth (the 'Anaths'), indicate that some of the beliefs and practices associated with these Baalaths or female consorts of Baal may also have been attached to the cult of Yahweh. A temple of Astarte, dating at least from the fourteenth century B.C., as well as numerous clay 'maisonettes' with representations of this goddess, have been discovered at *Beisân* (the ancient Beth-shean, south-east of Jezreel) by the Philadelphia Museum excavators (cf. 1 S 31^{10}). This temple was used by the Egyptians and later by the Philistines, who succeeded them in the possession of the town (*c.* 1172 B.C.), but it may also have been in use by the Israelites for some centuries after David captured the place (*c.* 1000 B.C.), and after it became tributary to Solomon.[1] At all events the existence of so much Baalism and Astartism within the Israelite territory must have affected the character of Yahwism. These heathen cults must have intermingled with it to a large extent, producing a syncretism in the religion of Israel. There was certainly much in common between them and it. The beliefs, social customs, and religious institutions of both had many points of agreement.

At the same time, in spite of all we have said, this apparent similarity between Baalism and Yahwism was largely superficial. There was clearly a deep distinction between the two; and though the barbarous customs of these other religions persisted in Yahwism, they were contrary to the moral sense of Israel. They were represented by Amos and Hosea as gross, sensual, and unworthy of a spiritual deity (Am $2^{7.8}$, Hos $4^{13.14}$). It was thoroughly injurious to have them established now in the royal household at Samaria, especially in pompous

[1] Cf. the *Museum Journal*, Sept. 1926, pp. 295 ff., and for a photograph of the interior of the temple, see *ibid.*, March 1927, p. 26.

Phœnician form, under the influence of Jezebel and her connections, and to have them planted among the people as national modes of worship. Baalism, whether Phœnician or not, was of agricultural origin, having to do specially with the soil. It was the Baal's province to give fertility to his own locality (to which he was strictly confined),[1] to help in the tilling of the fields, to produce the fruits of the land, and to water it from below or from above. Baalism was consequently debased with elements of nature-worship, accompanied with cruel rites and magic. By a process, to which we have abundant parallels in similar cults, it came also to have some connection with animal fruitfulness,[2] and was thus tainted with sensual passion and immorality. In Tyre and throughout Phœnicia it had grown into an idolatry of the most wanton character, directed by a numerous priesthood. One horrible feature of it there, inherited from the ancient Canaanites, was the offering up—generally by fire—of human sacrifices, especially of first-born children. The Phœnicians, who were conservative in religious matters, had retained this dreadful rite to its full extent. The Israelites, we know, were not altogether free from it. The story of the sacrifice of Isaac goes to show that it prevailed in Israel in early times. The history of Jephthah furnishes an in-

[1] Every district had its own Baal. The apparent oneness of Baal in the thoughts of some was an abstraction of later times.

[2] Cf. Nu $25^{1ff.}$; Kittel, *Geschichte des Volkes Israel*, 3rd ed., i. p. 218.

dubitable instance of it in the period of the Judges, and there are numerous prophetic references which seem to prove that it persisted in Israel till a late period (Mic 6^7, Jer 7^{31}, Ezk 20^{26} 23^{37}). But at the same time it was not an authorized part of the Mosaic cult, which rather taught that Yahweh was satisfied with the disposition that was prepared to offer to him one's dearest without requiring such an actual sacrifice. It was excluded from legitimate worship, being 'an alien element repudiated by conscious Yahwism.'[1] In the Phœnician worship, however, what Contenau calls 'l'horrible tare des sacrifices humains' persisted to a late period.[2] On ordinary occasions animals served as victims, but in times of public danger numbers of children were sacrificed under the idea that this averted calamity. The close relation that existed between Melḳart of Tyre and Baal-Ammon of Carthage (both known to the ancients as 'Moloch') testifies to the practice in Phœnicia.[3] At Carthage, on the site of the temple of Tanith, where four layers of urns have been unearthed containing a large number of calcined bones with some necklaces and amulets, a careful examination has proved that 85 per cent. are the bones of children offered to the gods.[4] At Gades

[1] Hölzinger on Gn $22^{14\text{-}20}$, quoted by Professor W. P. Paterson, *Hastings' Dict.*, iv. p. 334*b*.

[2] Contenau, *La Civilization phénicienne*, p. 137.

[3] Cf. Justin, xviii. 6, xix. i.

[4] E. Vassel et F. Icard, *Les Inscriptions votives du temple de Tanit à Carthage*, in *Revue Tunisienne*, 1923; R. Dussaud, *Trente-huit textes*

(modern *Cadiz*), a colony of Tyre, where the worship of Melḳart prevailed, the description we possess of the ritual shows that a perpetual fire burned in the temple, attended to by priests with shaven heads.[1] Horrible practices of this kind were undoubtedly out of harmony with the superior civilization of Phœnicia, but this fact only shows the intense vigour, militant and even fanatical, of the Phœnician religion, which could impose such rites on the people against their natural instinct. The worship of Astarte was specially revolting and dissolute. Lucian, for example, who visited the temple of Aphrodite in Byblus, describes the demoralizing accompaniments of the worship there (*De Dea Syria*, § 4); and in the temple at Aphaka in the Lebanon (at the source of the *Nahr-Ibrahim*), the rites practised were of such a character that they were suppressed by Constantine.[2]

In the Phœnician cults, too, there was a lack of social morality. It was out of the soil of Tyrian Baalism that the judicial murder of Naboth and his

puniques provenant du sanctuaire des ports à Carthage, in *Bulletin archéol.*, 1922.

[1] Contenau, *op. cit.* p. 139.

[2] Eusebius, *Vit. Const.* iii. 55; Döllinger, *Judenth. u. Heidenthum* (Eng. trans. by Darnell), i. pp. 425–429. The view of Contenau on this point is worth quoting (*La Civil. phén.*, p. 132): ‘Ce personnel des temples était complété par les hiérodules des deux sexes qui se livraient à la prostitution sacrée. Cette pratique est inséparable du culte d'Ashtart, grande déesse de la Fécondité. Nous connaissons mal le fonctionnement et la raison d'être de cette institution contre laquelle la Bible et les écrivains de l'Église se sont maintes fois élevés avec violence. Nous avons d'ailleurs sur ce point assez de témoignages concordants pour qu'il ne puisse être mis en doute.'

family grew. Ahab, to do him justice, gave up all thought of further action when he learned that Naboth had refused to part with his vineyard. It was at the instigation of his Tyrian wife, whose conceptions of morality were heathenish, that he ventured to permit the murder. The whole proceeding was a base iniquity, a thorough transgression of the eternal principles of justice and truth on which Yahwism was based, and probably it was not the only case in which the grosser conceptions of heathenism triumphed. It is quoted because it was the particular one which led to Elijah's protest. What stirred Yahweh's deepest anger was not any ritual offence, but rather oppression and cruelty. The teaching of Yahweh condemned the corrupt administration of the law, and called for justice in the gates. It protested against covetousness and greed, against luxurious living, and against the way in which the rich took advantage of their poorer neighbours, buying up their ground, joining field to field till there was no room in the land (Is 5[8]). It was otherwise with the licentious cults of Melḳart and Astarte; and Elijah realized that if these obtained a prominent place in Israel, the result would be a gigantic step downward, not only religiously but morally and socially. The dividing line between these cults and the purer worship of Yahweh might become less and less distinct, and the nation would suffer. What was to hinder Yahweh in course of time coming to be thought of as a kind of Tyrian Baal, no better than the sensuous and corrupt deities of other lands ?

Apart from these fundamental differences between the Phœnician and Israelite religions, Elijah no doubt felt strongly that the position of Yahweh as the sole God of Israel was being challenged. As a prophet of Yahweh, he resented the recognition within Israel, in any form, of the gods of other nations. Israel were the people of Yahweh. They had been chosen by Him ('You only have I known among all the families of the earth,' Am 3^{2}), brought out of Egypt by Him, led through the desert by Him, and their enemies had been cast out of the land by Him (Am 2^{10} 5^{25}). All Semitic religions were tribal or national. 'Thy people,' said Ruth, 'shall be my people, and thy God my God.' 'Hath any nation changed its god ?' asks Jeremiah (2^{11}). To be an Israelite and a worshipper of Yahweh was one and the same thing. The people and Yahweh formed together an important group, both being members, so to speak, of the same body or parts of one and the same organism (cf. Lv 25^{23}). There was a solidarity of the group ; the one could not exist without the other, and they were both bound up with the land they occupied.[1] Hence the unify-

[1] The Israelites applied this group idea to outside nations also. It is this idea that underlies the language of 1 S 26^{19}, where David's banishment from the ancestral domain is spoken of as involving the worship of other gods. The sphere of worship of a particular god extended over all the land of his people, but not beyond it. Other gods ruled outside. Hos $9^{3.4}$ assumes that no feast could be held in Yahweh's honour beyond the boundaries of Canaan ; and even a

ing conceptions which the Israelites had of national religion, government, and brotherhood, and hence also their ideas of rights, duties, and responsibilities. The nation, for instance, might suffer for the offence of any member (cf. Jos 7, Gn 20, 1 S 22, Mic 3^{12}), for the solidarity of the group was endangered in such a case, and the relations between the people and Yahweh were disturbed. About the time of the Exile this collective consciousness lost its strength (Ezk $18^{2ff.}$, La 5^{7}). The mass of people rose above it, and there were even approaches to a *Weltanschauung* which included the heathen nations in the scope of Yahweh's rule.[1] But later the idea of a national group responsibility returned and again ruled. It was this conception that led sometimes to a detestation of foreign alliance and showed itself in an antipathy to any relationship or form of civilization that exposed the people to outside cults.

The crisis that forced Elijah to take such stern measures was therefore of the gravest kind. The nation was at the parting of the ways, when it had to decide how its future was to be shaped. Whether Elijah was a monotheist or a mere champion of monolatry is uncertain. The probability is that monotheism was not explicitly asserted until the rise of Deutero-Isaiah. The vital issue with Elijah

post-exilic writer describes how Jonah took ship at Joppa, to flee 'from the presence of Yahweh.'

[1] Cf. Professor A. Causse, *Israël et la vision de l'humanité*, Strasbourg, 1924.

was whether Israel, who were the people of Yahweh, should serve the Tyrian Baal and other foreign cults, or should worship Yahweh. Elijah would have been lacking in faithfulness and moral courage if he had simply looked on while the nation was being drawn away from its God. The worship of the local Baalim or of the household deities, though bad enough, was a much smaller matter and on a lower plane, and was not conceived to be a serious infringement of the rights of Yahweh to the sole allegiance of His people. They stood in quite a different category from Yahweh, just as saints might receive homage different from that given to God alone. The case of Solomon, too, who arranged for his foreign wives worshipping their own deities in Jerusalem, was of a different type, for there seems to have been no effort to promote the worship of these deities among the people, though even here the prophetic party must have felt that Yahweh was outraged by the presence of these foreign cults, which were displaying themselves under the auspices of the king. The essence of the evil in Ahab's case lay not only in the corrupt nature of the Tyrian Baalism, but in the fact that the position of Yahweh, as sole God and ruler in the nation, was definitely challenged. Yahweh was either all or nothing: there could be no compromise. Ahab, no doubt, did not desire to expel Yahweh any more than Manasseh did, but only to set up the cults of Melḳart and Astarte at His side, mainly for political purposes. He did not meditate any apostasy. Far from that, he called his children Athaliah ('Yahweh is ruler'),[1] Ahaziah ('Yahweh is strong'), Jehoram ('Yahweh is high'), and Joash ('Yahweh is strong,' or 'Yahweh hath bestowed').[2] Even Jezebel did not seriously set herself to exterminate Yahweh's prophets, for there were no less than four hundred of them supporting Ahab when he started on his last expedition, and all, with one memorable exception, seemed to be eager for his success. Nevertheless, in spite of such allowances, Ahab's actions seriously affected the supremacy of Yahweh and the solidarity of Israel. He did more than merely tolerate the worship of Baal—he built in Samaria a temple and altar to Melḳart, in which a large number of orgiastic priests (probably Phœnician *Kohanim*) performed the same pagan ritual as in the great shrine at Tyre,[3] and he thus encouraged the active dissemination of such cults throughout the land. Jezebel doubtless wished devoutly for this latter consummation, and many a one, to gain her favour or in dread of her wrath,

[1] The name seems to be a compound of Yah with the Assyrian *etillu* (=Sumerian NIR), 'ruler' or 'lord.' See Muss-Arnolt, *Reference Glossary*, p. 381*a*, and Prince, *Sumerian Lexicon*, p. 263, l. 1.

[2] For the name Joash, cf. Hommel, *Expos. Times*, viii. (1897), p. 562.

[3] The words in 1 K 18^{19}, 'and the prophets of the Ashera 400,' are probably an interpolation. They do not occur in v.^{40}, nor in the Massoretic text of v.^{22}. Cf. Robertson Smith, *Religion of the Semites*, 2nd ed., p. 189; Wellhausen, *Die Composition des Hexateuchs*, pp. 285 f.; Klostermann, *Die Bücher Samuelis und der Könige*, p. 367; Kittel, in Kautzsch, *Die heilige Schrift des Alten Testaments*, p. 94.

may have supported her. As a natural result, Yahweh's altars were thrown down (1 K 18[30] 19[14]), His sacrifices ceased here and there, and many of His faithful people were driven into obscurity. The prophetic protest was crushed out, and Elijah, its leading exponent, was expelled. Judging from the names of Ahab's stewards and the consigners of wine and oil which occur on the *ostraka*, one would conclude that Yahweh was still popular—perhaps more popular than Baal. The total number of names occurring is not less than 52, of which 11 are Yahweh names (namely, Shemaryo, Gaddiyo, Bedyo (?), Yedaʿyo, ʿAbedyo, Marnayo (occurring twice, different men), ʿEgelyo, Abiyo (? Ariyo), Yo-yada, and Yo-yosheb), while only 6 are compounded with Baal (namely, Baalzamar, Baalazkar, Baalmeʿoni, Meribaal, Abibaal, and Baala). But no conclusion can be drawn from such a fact, for these stewards and others were grown-up men, and their name must have been given some years before Ahab ascended the throne. For a correct judgment on such a matter, one would require the names of those born during his reign.[1] Further, we cannot conclude, from the fact that a single temple held all the Tyrian Baal worshippers in the time of Jehu (2 K 10[21]), that the same was true in the days of Ahab. For the number of such

[1] In Israelite times, names were given, as a rule, immediately after birth, and only in very special cases was the name changed in mature life. Cf. Buchanan Gray, *Hastings' Dict.*, iii. p. 480 f.

worshippers must have decreased under Jehoram, the son of Ahab, who opposed the foreign cult (2 K 3²), and it is not likely, moreover, that all the devotees of Baal had such faith in Jehu as to accept his invitation to the temple.

Where Ahab erred was in his *policy*. He had made an alliance with Phœnicia, but the drawback was that it invited on his part an official recognition of the Phœnician cult, and he felt that he must be guided in such a matter, not by the requirements of Yahweh's prophets, but by the dictates of political prudence. He felt that it would not do to be intolerant, and was willing to have a compromise by which the worship of Baal and of Yahweh could be practised together. It has been said in his defence that he could not be expected to see things with the illumination of a prophet, nor to realize, as later historians might do, the serious issues resulting from an alliance that appeared so advantageous at the time. Still, he could not but know that as king he was head and representative of the people. In a sense peculiar to ancient monarchs in theocratic nations, he was head both of the religious and of the political organizations. Temple and palace were connected, and he virtually controlled both. As king, he had remarkable powers and special responsibilities, and more than any ordinary member of the Israelite group he could bring guilt upon the nation (cf. David, 2 S 24[17]; Manasseh, Jer 15[4]; the priest, Lv 4[3]). He was in a sense the sole actor, and his actions were essentially those of the nation, in the same way as the deeds of a bedouin sheikh were regarded as those of the tribe. The king and the kingdom were one (cf. Ezk 28–32, Is 14$^{4-21}$, where the kings of Tyre, Egypt, etc., and their peoples are included together). It was thus a mistaken policy of Ahab to do anything that might detract from the supremacy of Yahweh, the One God of Israel. Hosea at a later time laid emphasis on the same point. His writings show that he was opposed on religious grounds to such compromises. He regarded diplomacy of this kind as foolish, for it made Israel the prey of her foes (Hos 7$^{11ff.}$), and it was false and treacherous (10$^{4ff.}$). It is evident that Ahab's policy, which connived too much at the conduct of his unscrupulous wife, entirely justified the condemnation of Elijah and the efforts of the prophetic school to suppress it, and to bring in a purer Yahwism, free from Baalism, Astartism, and foreign evils. The movement under Elijah, indeed, appears inexplicable if there were not flagrant evils sufficient to offend the religious conceptions of the prophets.

That Elijah and even the revolutionary Jehu did not succeed in freeing the land from a corrupt worship is due to the fact that Israel's religious conceptions were far more deeply permeated with 'heathenism' than those of Judah were. There seems to have been a set-back in the worship of the Tyrian Baal according to indisputable facts in the later history, but otherwise Baalism continued to pollute the land. Israel claimed to represent the proper continuation of the Solomonic empire—a claim which was drastically expressed by King Joash (2 K 14^9). This was probably justified in the political sphere, for she inherited the chief strength of the nation. But in the religious sphere she could hardly be called the heir of the ancient traditions. Her religious ideas and cult, as we have pointed out, were far removed from a consistent henotheism. There is abundant evidence in Amos, the shepherd of Tekoa (*c.* 760 B.C., during the reign of Jeroboam II.), the first of the great prophets whose writings have survived, to show that, in spite of Elijah's protests and the reforms which took place at different times, her worship of Yahweh continued full of imitations of Phœnician and Canaanite practices. One must of course remember the peculiar standpoint of Amos. His ideal of life was almost entirely pastoral or agricultural, involving an existence in which there were no cities, no regular army, no central power, no court or aristocracy, no commerce or luxury, and in which there was a simple form of worship without temple or altar or priestly caste. His philosophy was undeveloped, and his theology was contradictory and saturated in old mythological ideas. But even though we make large deductions for all this, there is sufficient evidence in his trenchant criticism to prove that a century after Elijah the worship of Yahweh was still pagan and polluted.

A little later, judging from the references in Hosea (*c.* 750 B.C.), who knew the northern kingdom intimately, the struggle as to whether Baal was going to displace Yahweh in the thoughts and affections of the people appears to have been still going on in full strength. It was not a mere question of forms and ceremonies; it was rather a question as to whether the fruits of the earth were the gift of the Baalim or of Yahweh, whether the one was to be acknowledged as God or the other. There seems to have been a constant life and death conflict between the two conceptions, and this continued to be the case during the whole period of the monarchy, although some of the priests and kings co-operated with the prophets.

The fact is that, owing to her northern position, Israel had become more and more involved in the politics of other nations, such as Assyria. This brought her into contact with their gods, who often appeared immensely powerful and superior. 'For us, alliance with a foreign power, even when the nation which seeks the alliance is in need of help, leaves the inner ideals of the dependent people uninfluenced except in subtle ways which are difficult to trace. But in that early time, dependence on the foreigner inevitably brought with it some recognition of the religion of the superior State.'[1] The result was that Israel was tempted involuntarily to depreciate the power of Yahweh, and as a conse-

[1] Welch, *The Religion of Israel under the Kingdom*, p. 116.

quence to despise Yahweh Himself. One can easily understand that such a religion was no help to the moral strength of the people. There was almost constant strife of factions, led by revolutionary leaders who sought to glut the greed and vengeance of their partisans, and one dynasty after another rose in impotent violence and then fell a prey to assassination. The foundations of the old life began to break up. Externally the state was prosperous, especially in the reign of Jeroboam II., but this prosperity covered an abyss of social disorder. There was a rottenness beneath the brilliance. The great farmers no longer lived among the peasantry and laboured along with them. The connection with Phœnicia, which had opened up a profitable foreign market for their agricultural produce (Ezk 27^{17}), had made them rich merchants and forestallers of grain (Am 8^{5}, Hos 12^{7}). Wealth began to accumulate in a few hands, to the corresponding impoverishment of the others, while constant exportation raised the price of the necessaries of life.[1] The mass of the people were loaded with debt and were taken advantage of on all hands. Every kind of vice flourished luxuriantly. The well-to-do, who were revelling in luxury, oppressed the poor and grew fat upon the misery of others, pride and rapacity prevailed, the laws of justice were openly perverted, self-indulgence and moral corruption were every-

[1] Cf. Robertson Smith, *The Old Testament in the Jewish Church*, p. 347.

where visible. We hear no more of seven thousand who had not bowed the knee to Baal. Hosea ($4^{1ff.}$) is constrained to lament that there was no fidelity, no love, no knowledge of God, no spirituality in the land. The degeneration into which the nation was falling wrought its effects in due time. In 722 B.C., after a long and despairing struggle, the northern kingdom fell before the conquering armies of Sargon.

GENERAL INDEX

NOTE.—In this Index, the alphabetical arrangement ignores such prefixes as Mt., *Tell* ('mound'), *Wady* ('torrent,' 'valley'), *Beit* ('house'), *Kefr*, *Kafr* ('village'), *Khurbet* ('ruin'), *Nahr* ('river'), and the Arabic article (*el-*). Modern place-names are in italics.

The Biblical references are placed separately (p. 172).

Abel Beth-Maʿakah, 83.
Abel Meḥolah, 93.
Abîbaʿal, inscription of, 44, 55.
Abiʿezer, 69, 71, 76, 78, 86, 99.
Abisaros, 71.
Âbl, 83.
Adad-idri II., 3, 23, 114, 119 n. 3, 120 ff., 129.
Adad-nirari, 124.
Administrative districts, Ahab's, 85 ff.; Judah's, 103 ff.; *vide* also Districts.
Adoram, 24.
Afis, stele at, 123.
el-ʿAfûleh, 73.
Ahab, date of reign, 6; Naboth's vineyard, 2; his civilizing work, 6; his levies, 24; his palace, 16 ff.; his administrative system, 85 ff.; his luxury, 101; his foreign policy, 106 ff.; his religious policy, 158; religious situation under, 132 ff.; pro-Assyrian, 122 ff.; his death, 23, 125, 128; Judæan estimate of, 108, 130 f., 133 f.
Ahaz, king of Judah, 124.
Ahaziah, king of Israel, 20.
Ahinoʿam, steward, 87; district of, 99.
Aḫîrâm, inscription on tomb, 53 f.
Aijalon, vale of, 65 f.; town, 92.
Albright, Dr. W. F., 70, 77, 86, 89 n. 1, 95.
Alphabet, *Serâbit*, 51 f.; Phœnician, 36 f., 44 f., 46 n. 3, 52 ff., 60 ff.; of *ostraka*, 43; cursive, 45; Greek, 46; Northern Semitic, 46 ff.; Table of, 164.
el-Amarna Letters, 54, 61 f., 70.
Amatha, 81.
Amatin, 76.
Amos, 101, 112, 132, 148, 160.
Anastasi IV., papyrus, 32; I. papyrus, 60, 70, 82, 118.
Anāthôth, 147.
ʿAnzah (*ʿAnazah*), 75.
Apamea, 126.
Aphaka, temple at, 151.
Aphek, 120, 125.
Aphraia, 74.
ʿArabah, 73.
Aramæans, 68, 97; wars with Israel, 106, 117, 124; league against Assyria, 120 ff.
Argob, 94.
Armôn, 20.
ʿArrâbeh, 73, 92.
Arrow-heads, iron, 31.
Arruboth (Arubboth), 73, 92, 97.
Art, Israelite, 25 ff.
Article, Hebrew definite, 57.
ʿAsharot, 75.
Asher, district of, 95 f.
Ashērā, 145; prophets of, 156 n. 3.
Ashtôreth, 143 n. 1, 147.
Ashur-naṣir-pal II., 117, 119, 121.
Ashur-uballit I., 114.

INDEX OF TEXTS CITED OR ILLUSTRATED

INDEX OF HEBREW TERMS

PRINTED BY
MORRISON AND GIBB LTD.
EDINBURGH AND LONDON